Dear AMAZING Leslie,
   There aren't enough words to
express my deep gratitude for your
generous and transformative love, care,
acceptance, and countless gifts ♡

SOUNDPATH

May you have many sound blessings,
   Peaceful harmony and
   much love,

Karen Olson ♡

KAREN OLSON, PH.D.

SoundPath Disclaimers

This publication contains the opinions and ideas of its author. It is intended to provide helpful and informative material on the subject addressed in the book. The author and publisher do not engage in rendering medical help or any other kind of personal professional services in the book. The reader should consult his or her medical health or other competent professional. The author is not responsible for any liability associated with the contents of this book.

To retain anonymity, the names and identifying details have been changed.

Published by

© 2018 Karen Olson
Contributing Editor: Kuwana Haulsey

The author gratefully acknowledges permission to reprint photos from: *Cymatics: A Study of Wave Phenomena and Vibration*, by Dr. Hans Jenny. © 2001 MACROmedia Publishing, Eliot, ME, USA. www.cymaticsource.com.

Photo Credit: Chakra Chart—3xy

Back Page Photo Credit: Sam Kahn/Imageworks NYC

ISBN Harcover: 978-1-64184-937-1
ISBN Paperback: 978-1-64184-938-8
ISBN Ebook: 978-1-64184-939-5

ACKNOWLEDGMENTS

I feel like a conductor looking at the faces of the orchestra members who helped me compose this book. Beautiful harmonies are evoked as the group is united to help the conductor and the composer express the music's message and contribute their unique input to create a rich sound. This has been my turn. We can stand and look out together as we experience the audience's thunderous applause, and all of our energies join together in appreciation. What a glorious opportunity has been given me—to bring this book, truly a dream, into the world with the support of so many who join me in knowing how many more I can help with my healing message.

As I see the different sections of the orchestra, I look to each group and ask them to bow. I applaud and thank each person from my heart and offer a prayer for added blessings.

My standing ovation begins with my family for their love, support, patience, and for being my invaluable teachers: my husband Beau; and my children, Lisette and Scott, who bring me my greatest joy. Love to my mom and dad for teaching me and showing me what love, faith, passion, perseverance, and dedication is. I thank my sister Mary and my brother Dave and their families for being what a family is all about: love.

There are many more; each person knows the ways they have helped me. A huge heartfelt applause for William Kelly Milionis, Mary Adams, Ayme Turnbull, Beth Grossman, Claire Faithful, Jacob Barrocas, Joe Gauld, Tony Camacho, and Jeff Volk.

I offer enormous gratitude to my gifted editor Donna Mosher, who masterfully pulled it all together so that the music could sing and the meaning could be heard; and for Mitch Rudman's help while the book was still just a dream. A special thank you to Chris O'Bryne and his team at JetLaunch for skillfully taking care of the details of reality.

With continued thanks for God's grace, miracles, and gifts.

Karen Olson, Ph.D.

CONTENTS

INTRODUCTION

We experience sound before we are born, and it carries us beyond the veil as we transition from this life. We hear a symphony of sounds in our mother's womb, with the surrounding fluid magnifying and transmitting the vibrations into our cells. Our mother's heartbeat, her breathing, and the pulsation of blood swooshes a rhythmic pulse, which peacefully accompanies the building of our cells and organs. Our parents' voices and the sounds of our mother's day-to-day life make up our interior world from the very beginning of our time on earth.

As we go through the various stages of life, our body stores our experiences in a manner more primal than language and explanation. If something traumatic happens, and it seems to be more than we can handle, we create internal protections. These protections can help at that moment, but then that pattern becomes instilled, stored, and stuck inside of us on a deep subconscious level. We need to unlearn and replace these defense mechanisms.

SoundPath exercises help us to reach below the conscious mind, below language and explanation, to use "ultrasonic surgery" to dislodge old patterns. Then, we can fill those stuck and empty spaces with unconditional love, reconnecting to the place we remember subconsciously in our mother's womb—that place where all our needs were met, where we were enough and knew that we were loved.

Even if there were times when we couldn't receive this fully as a child, we can do it now. We can reset to our pre-trauma state. That trauma doesn't have to be a huge incident that appeared in the newspaper. We can experience chronic trauma over time—constant put-downs, feeling unsupported, or being subjected to any behavior that made us feel unnurtured, unloved or unaccepted by our "tribe."

We innately know that we were born to fit in and be cared for. We know that we are unique and special. I believe that even though trauma may have drowned out that message, it remains underneath the chaos and is always there for us to reconnect with.

Your soul knows and never forgets the truth of who you are and what you are here to do. You are seeking this connection. This is the quiet voice which SoundPath can help you to hear.

The SoundPath principles allow us to tune in to higher vibrations so we can co-create a new lifestyle based on faith instead of fear, trust instead of doubt, and harmony instead of discord. Tuning up the mind and body creates balance and a renewed sense of clarity.

If you've gone through life feeling like you're not enough or striven to earn the approval of others—the SoundPath tools will raise your confidence and increase your peace of mind.

ABOUT SOUNDPATH

SoundPath provides a method to gain insight and to learn vibrational tools that access the subconscious mind and the brain's ability to reprogram pathways within itself—opening up new channels to a life filled with ease, harmony, happiness, and success. These vibrational tools often involve music, or at the very least, rhythm. However, no specific knowledge of music or rhythm is required. The SoundPath method is flexible enough to adapt to one's own preferences and tastes.

Let's begin by looking at the concept that humans are instruments that need to be kept "in tune" in order to achieve the best results. Most people—even those with no musical training at all—can recognize when a singer is out of tune. Fortunately, most people's lives are not so far "out of tune" as to be beyond help—if they understand some basic concepts and implement the right corrective measures.

Fundamental to the SoundPath method are some lofty scientific principles, but again they need not be thoroughly studied nor completely understood. We just need to know enough to be able to use them to reach our own self-improvement goals. Like gravity, we only need to know that it works. We can leave it up to the experts to debate about *how* it works.

Among those experts is Bruce Lipton, Ph.D., who made groundbreaking discoveries about the role of the conscious versus the subconscious minds, as outlined in his book: *The Biology of Belief: Unleashing the Power of Conscious Matter and Miracles.* It has been shown that only about five percent of what we do is controlled by our conscious minds. And, considering that much of what we observe and experience in our lives today is related to the behavior of our parents who had modeled for us what they themselves had learned at a young age…it could be stated that we behave more out of habit than choice. Lipton's concepts, when effectively applied, have the potential to change lives. We no longer have to passively watch our own stubborn patterns accelerate and repeat in mysterious and "unfair" ways.

Scientists used to believe that our genetics determined our fate. But, now we understand that our genes act as a blueprint that receive programming based on observation and the experience of repeated behaviors. After age seven, *our programming controls our genes!* The programs have been "auto-saved," becoming our very own GPS—our personal navigational reference system. When our subconscious mind is running the show, we tend to be unaware of it, so we can easily believe that we are victims. But, we don't need to pass along all of our ancestor's habits and beliefs. We *do* have a choice!

The first step in this reprogramming process is gaining awareness. Usually, our minds are in "la-la land" while we unknowingly sabotage ourselves. What the conscious mind wishes is very different than the wishes of the subconscious mind. It's like the unconscious mind is in the driver's seat while the conscious mind occasionally barks an unheard order from the back seat. The subconscious mind doesn't like to change. Our best chance for creating new subconscious patterns is when we're in a meditative or Theta brainwave state; just before we fall asleep and wake up is an optimal time to "rehearse" the changes we want.

From an energetic and vibrational standpoint, music allows the spiritually connected listener to have more direct contact with one's subconscious programming. I see this regularly as I practice and teach the viola. I can remember the tedious hours, days, and weeks I would spend, trying to learn a new way to hold my bow or align my left-hand finger motion until it became a part of my playing without my thought. Of course, I used the new "habit" over and over again, so it automatically received consistent reinforcement.

This principle and the process of creating new habits are very apparent when I am teaching a proper bow-arm technique to my students. The right arm motion is not at all natural. The elbow needs to learn to open at a right angle and extend to keep the bow parallel to the bridge so it can create a ringing sound. When the bow goes "off course" the sound gets thin, glassy, unpleasant—sounding almost like a whistle. We can work very hard to break that habit. Yet, if we are focusing on a difficult left-hand technique, for instance, the bow will wander back to its old habit. I have learned very well that we need to focus on one task at a time until the mind can gradually put it all together. There is no need to become disappointed when the bow begins to wander again. But, it is a reminder that the consistent work isn't complete, as the new habit has yet to fully replace the old. Even once it has become a habit, it's still important to warm up each day, like an athlete, to provide the proper reinforcement.

If the conscious mind has barely a five percent impact on the choices we make and the situations that manifest in our experience, how do we bypass it and communicate directly with the subconscious mind? Even the attempt to make a change in the conscious mind, often only reinforces the problem we're trying to solve. SoundPath will give you a way to establish direct communication with your subconscious mind and bring into awareness your core beliefs. The tools and exercises in this book will explain how to use sound therapy and specific vibratory frequencies—along with more traditional methods of self-healing, like meditation—to create positive change down to the cellular level by reprogramming subconscious beliefs.

You can choose to move on from feeling stuck, in pain, grief-stricken, or hopelessness. New patterns *can* finally be established. Past situations no longer need to influence the present moment; now you'll have a way to move forward and freely choose to live your dreams.

The SoundPath exercises presented here will often include using your imaginative sense, like daydreaming, to create an experience as if it is real. The subconscious mind does not fully distinguish between what is experienced and what is imagined. We can choose to use this ability to our advantage. For example, you will be asked to imagine the vibrations inside of you, similar to when you stand near a huge loudspeaker with pounding bass notes that shake within you. The energetic messages to the subconscious mind are felt; they can be perceived physically, or through guided imagery, just below the threshold of your thinking, conscious mind.

As our connection to the energy fields of sound and music helps us use these exercises and gain knowledge to implement change, we become progressively clearer and more vibrant. When our body, mind, and spirit, are in alignment, our body knows how to heal and achieve optimal health. In this state, we are able to magnify the results of all our desires, including medical care and optimal health. Our higher level of vibration helps us to sing from the mountaintops, as the resonant sound echoes our symphony of support. Learning the SoundPath method does not include one-time moments of awareness that are then forgotten and discarded. Instead, it can become a "way of life" that includes ongoing maintenance exercises, similar to getting and keeping your physical body in shape rather than dieting only to blindly return to a former lifestyle.

Spiritually speaking, when our instrument is in tune, the overtones are all ringing and resonating in agreement. In other words, our relationships are whole and healthy; our finances are abundant; we have the courage and the passion for living our purpose; we experience high self-esteem and joyful self-expression. However, if the instrument is unbalanced or out of tune, it isn't effective on any level. The sound is terrible. No matter how skilled the musician, it can't be played effectively, and trying to do so is a miserable experience.

Likewise, when a person is "out of tune," he or she will experience symptoms such as anxiety, insecurity, doubt, shame, blame, jealousy, and addiction. Such a person is prone to seeking direction and approval from others. Life feels unnecessarily difficult; things often go wrong, and accidents happen far too frequently. Intimate relationships are tarnished with disagreements. And, since schedules tend to be hectic, it can become difficult to care for one's physical needs like eating well, exercising, or getting enough sleep. Most challenging of all, it may feel impossible to get control over negative core beliefs that magnify these struggles. This is certainly the opposite of being in the flow and having things come together with joy, happiness, and ease. *It is our lifelong imperative to get our instruments in tune.*

So how do we do this? How can we create harmony and alignment between the player and the instrument which will restore balance and allow our music to ring out freely? How do we release the chaos of negative core beliefs that may have haunted us throughout our lives despite our best efforts to change?

As with any instrument, making the right adjustments is crucial. We must learn specific practices which will keep our instrument tuned so we can experience all that life has to offer. The process of tuning up our "instrument" is remarkably similar to the experience of a musician tuning a physical instrument. And, it all comes down to sound and vibration.

SoundPath shows us how to become master musicians for our own emotional and spiritual awakening. These techniques will demonstrate ways to combine vibration, entrainment, tapping, and drumming, with techniques like meditation, breath work, intention-setting, and movement, to bypass subconscious blocks. These blocks keep us reliving the same negative experiences over and over again, regardless whether we "know better by now" or have struggled to overcome the same challenges for many years.

I don't need to tell you that music can affect our moods, emotions, and even our bodies. But, most of us are less familiar with other ways that music has played a pivotal role in human social and emotional development throughout recorded history. From Paleolithic flutes carved more than forty thousand years ago to Native Americans ritual songs for everything from marriage celebrations to war, music has long been understood to be a mystical force in our world.

There are extreme examples of using music to create trance states so deep that people in India have reported being bitten by cobras without experiencing illness. Prisoners of war have endured terrible abuse such as starvation and physical injury using humming and singing as a technique to focus the mind beyond the pain. And, we all know people, *you* may even be one of those people, who've come through a time of depression or trauma by focusing on a piece of music that spoke to them giving courage to keep moving forward.

There's music within each of us, waiting to be awakened. You must allow that music to come to you because gifts that aren't shared will eventually disappear. Gifts we share are multiplied. Memories of pain we keep reliving can be healed and released, allowing us to move forward and make more joyful memories. This vibrational memory can carry us to higher places where we no longer allow anger, negativity, and fear to steal our gifts from us.

Instead of resigning ourselves to more years of struggle, we can use sound to cut a new pathway through our subconscious blocks, finally healing lifelong negative core beliefs. This is a new concept for most people, but it isn't nearly as far-fetched as it may appear at first glance. The famed scientist Nikola Tesla said, "If you want to find the secrets of the universe, think in terms of energy, frequency, and vibration."

There's a power greater than our problems. Sound opens our consciousness to reflect it. SoundPath offers the tools to create effective, lasting change. So, let's learn to think in sound. Let rhythm be our inner pulse connecting us to universal life. Let the music lead us to our inner story.

ONE
The Missing Notes

Though love expresses itself in many forms, types, and flavors, it flows from just one source. Love is the universal language through which we communicate with our Higher Power; it offers peace in the face of conflict and wholeness that mends the broken places in our hearts. Love smooths away the pain that arises when negative core beliefs hold undue influence over our day-to-day choices, affecting the way we see ourselves and our place in the world.

We learn the language of love from parents and caregivers. But, sometimes that language is missing the necessary vocabulary or hasn't been transmitted clearly enough to be understood and received. When that happens, it can leave holes in our understanding of love that must be filled in later if we're ever going to fully participate in a rich and meaningful life. These holes act like missing notes in a musical composition; they leave blank spaces that may seem undetectable at first but interrupt the flow and harmony in the life that's being created.

People often misunderstand what these holes, or missing notes mean and where they come from. We mistakenly believe that there's something inherently missing from inside *us*, not simply a glitch in our understanding. Far too often, people try to fill the holes that they feel on the inside with external experiences, people, or things. We want to look perfect, like we have it all together, so that no one suspects there's uncertainty roiling beneath the surface.

Though it's often, correctly, mentioned that perfection is unobtainable, we can still look around and see the lives of others are practically oozing with success and perfection. Those people seem to have produced many 10s on their scorecard of life. They look happy, fulfilled, and loved. They seem complete. Yet, no matter how perfect we may appear, life will test us all. It will expose the holes and deficiencies that we try so hard to mask. Inevitably, life will get interrupted and changes will occur that can never be undone, even with the most perfect of efforts.

Digging into the deepest soil from which we are grown brings up mental images of weeds, roots, worms, and rocks, hidden in the darkened earth. Turning the earth can seem like messy work. But, it's necessary so that what we're destined to grow into can take root and be born. It allows us to become attuned to that which holds the essence of our being; it's the perfectly imperfect work of learning to love ourselves unconditionally. In other words, you can't sing your full melody or be who you truly are while believing that something fundamental is missing from you.

Living life from a place of unconditional self-love is a wonderful goal. It doesn't mean being perfect or without flaw. It means speaking a language of love that knows more compassion than judgment, more self-forgiveness than animosity. It means knowing that your missing notes can be written in by a loving hand.

Tapping into this source of energy feels like you're in a flow. Things come together with ease and grace. You have synchronicity. You genuinely feel happiness, and you often find yourself laughing. You have energy, feel motivated, enjoy helping others, and are discerning about when it isn't best to do so. You are creative and open to unique ideas. You're able to love freely, forgive, and move on from challenges. Of course, in the balance of life, there will be times when you don't feel all of that. But, having an awareness of what seems off and then knowing how to shift it helps shorten the difficult periods.

The alternative, trying to fill our perceived "holes" with other things or people, never ends well. It invariably leads to feelings of inadequacy because we're always looking for something to fill the void: our parents' approval and acceptance, romantic love, financial success, etc. If we don't feel like we're enough, that lack presents itself in many different forms. Addiction, victimhood, not making healthy choices, worry and anxiety, fear of loss, and self-sabotage are just a few.

Some people believe that it's practically impossible to grow up completely free of the latent insecurities or emotional holes that create the internal voice of "not enough." But, I've met people who grew up with incredibly loving, respectful, and supportive parents who were well-balanced and kind by nature. These were parents who wanted each of their children to find their passion with their full support and without trying to control what that expression would look like. So, I do believe that it's possible to grow up in an environment that's conducive to developing wholeness and fulfillment within the family.

I will admit that I haven't met a large number in this category, and there's a part of me that is amazed when I'm around them. Due to my upbringing, I'm not in this category. In fact, feeling "not enough" has always been one of my major, reoccurring challenges. But, now I understand that when something happens to trigger those old feelings of inadequacy, I can make the choice to shift that energy and focus on the truth that is present in any given situation: *my Higher Power is the source of all love, including me; I am in harmony with the unconditional love and perfection that binds the universe together. There are no empty spaces or missing notes in me.*

You can't sing your full melody or be who you were born to be while believing that something fundamental is missing from you. Trying to do so reminds me of the image of a sail without wind. The vastness of the ocean is laid out before you, but you can't go anywhere. It's imperative to know the value of who you are and what you do.

One of the most significant violinists of our time, Joshua Bell, participated in an experiment. He played his violin just outside a subway station with over a thousand-people passing by. Barely a handful of people noticed him or seemed to enjoy his playing. In the forty-five minutes he played, only six people stopped to listen. About twenty people absently tossed him money as they continued to walk past. He collected a few dollars and change. No one applauded or gave him any special recognition. Yet, he had played masterfully on a three-million-dollar violin, the Gibson ex Huberman, handcrafted in 1713 by Antonio Stradivari. Just two days earlier, he had played the same pieces, except that it was to a sold-out audience who paid an average of one hundred dollars per ticket.

What made the difference?

Could that experiment have changed Joshua's opinion of how he played—his value, his worth or the importance of what he did? With all his success, and knowing that it was just an experiment, probably not. But, how many times does the average person "perform" to a less-than-enthusiastic audience—whether it be a work presentation, on a date, or when trying anything new—and feel judged by the reactions? How many times do we judge ourselves as "less than" or unworthy when the responses from others don't live up to our expectations?

We can learn so much from this story, which was shared by the Pulitzer-winning writer, Gene Weingarten. What I took from it was to always focus on doing my best. How it's received isn't my responsibility. My only job is to trust in myself, do my best, and stay in the present moment. Because, as Gene Weingarten asked, "If people don't have a moment to stop and listen to some of the best music played by one of the best musicians in the world, how many other moments have we missed?"

Ask yourself how this example might apply to you—your jobs, activities, goals, or experiences? How many times have you let failure or a fear of a negative reaction hold you back from accomplishing a goal? Have potentially sublime moments passed you by? Or, worse yet, have the missing notes in your own life become hiding places for unresolved fear or pain?

For me, the feeling of being misunderstood and "not enough" was a type of chronic pain. I searched to become whatever I thought would resolve that pain, whatever was needed for me to be deemed worthy enough to be loved. That need to feel loved unconditionally and validated became almost like an addiction. I don't use the term *addict* in a judgmental way because it's not about fault. Being an addict isn't solely about taking drugs or alcohol. If we have a void that makes us feel like we're unworthy, it causes us to try to fill the emptiness at all costs. This is the genesis of any addiction.

This is what happens when people are co-dependent, addicted to trying to "save" a loved one, living through other people, believing you need someone else to help you be enough, develop eating disorders, shop excessively, have unsafe sexual practices, and the list goes on. People are trying to fill a void that can only be filled by our connection to a Higher Power. Through this connection, we're finally able to find our answers. The answer is not to make any person, place, or thing, into a Higher Power. Doing so only prevents our ability to grow and find the truth within.

A powerful process that helps release our attachment to any addiction is to acknowledge the significant role that it has played in our lives. It is built into our defense mechanisms to make us feel safe, to give the appearance of having more control, and to distract us from our fears and uncertainties.

SoundPath Vibrational Therapy is an incredibly useful tool to help us to heal and shift into a new level of certainty that we are enough and that we have enough. It helps us make the transition from sharing with others from guilt or obligation to sharing from the overflow of our goodness. We realize that it's no longer necessary to give at our own expense. When you do something from a sense of lack or neediness, it simply creates a greater sense of need. It seems as if your effort will fill the lack, but it does the opposite; it makes you believe that you need the validation more. It's as if when you get what you want, it comes as a debt. And, the interest payment on this debt is so high that the principal amount can never be paid in full. It is a hidden trick that increases your sense of scarcity and low self-esteem.

For me, trying to fill my missing notes manifested as an overwhelming need to help others. It's complicated because I genuinely and innately love to help others, so the impulse always came with a pure intention. But, the subconscious beliefs that turned my desire into something unhealthy, remained hidden until I began to dig and look for answers. I realized that part of my desire to help came from my feelings of unworthiness. I needed to serve others—not just to uplift them, but to even be considered a viable human being, friend, or partner.

But, when I came to a relationship with my "hidden holes showing," I put myself in a position of being energetically "less than." As a result, people would often take advantage of me in some way. Some would take me for granted, use me to get ahead, disregard my contributions, or behave in disrespectful, degrading, or demanding ways. It was painful for me to finally admit to myself that these behaviors were a reflection of what I believed about myself.

Sometimes, I would even join in and continue this negative line of thinking, almost like I was on "their side," instead of sticking up for myself and claiming my worth. In fact, even after I'd done something well, if there was one thing that I believed could have been better, I would beat myself up about it afterward, feeling tormented and terrible. I was trying to fill in my missing notes by creating more pain for myself because it was a feeling that I was already used to and almost comfortable with, in a way. That low vibration energy had come to define me.

Fortunately, that game is finally over! Now, I'm on my side, meaning that I love and support myself. I understand the folly of seeking something that's impossible to obtain from an external source; this unsuccessful seeking causes us to seek it even more, and this desire continues to increase as the destruction it causes also increases. This cycle is challenging for a person to see when they are caught up in it.

When someone is stuck in the cycle of trying to fill in their missing notes in impossible ways, there are usually three fundamental core beliefs that need to be checked and shifted:

1. I am worthy of God's love. (I choose to call my Higher Power "God".

2. I am worthy of unconditional love.

3. I am worthy of an instant healing.

Let's look at the first statement: "I am worthy of God's love." Ask yourself: are you able to say, and believe, the following words: "I don't need to earn love. I deserve to be happy and healthy and successful. I have God's perspective on who I am and on everything that has happened to me. I deserve to have all my needs met. I am worthy to be of service to others and live a life of purpose." Knowing God's love is about knowing your oneness with life itself, that goodness and beauty abound throughout all of God's creation, and that includes you.

The next statement, "I am worthy of unconditional love," is similar to the first, but pertains directly to our ability to accept love from others. Human relationships can be fraught with pitfalls, uncertainty, heartbreak, and unmet needs. Ask yourself if you've created a life surrounded by people who love and accept you just the way you are. Do they maintain a relationship with you based on unconditional love or because of what you have and what you can do?

Finally, the statement "I am worthy of instant healing" refers to our ability to tap into our connection with all that is—the universal good that underlies all creation. Nothing is impossible, and no problem is too great to solve when we're at one with this healing force. Miracles can happen when we connect to the source of our good.

Recently, as I sat in meditation, I had an insight into the nature of universal love. I closed my eyes, cleared my mind, followed my breath, and watched any thoughts that floated by. After a while,

I felt a connection to a core strand, a vibrating "string," that felt connected to "All That Is". I could feel the earth, the heavens, the cells in my body orchestrated to the strand that was the main "conductor" of the symphony. I could feel myself become aligned with the Creator, my Higher Self, as I let go and released what had caused dissonance. I felt my soul beneath the cells that I am comprised of; I felt love holding it all together. It was simple. It was peace. It was everything.

The impetus for this experience was when I needed to prepare to say goodbye to my dad who was in his final weeks. At first, my mind was filled with anger and details of what I had missed from my dad in my childhood and throughout my life. Then, one day, by the grace of God, I was given this gift of peace, and I experienced the deep love beneath all of the circumstances and unimportant frailties of our limited lives.

My dad passed away about three months later. Thinking about this meditation reminds me of the gift of grace I was given one day. My dad was a sincere spiritual seeker. His unparalleled dedication and life of service changed the lives of thousands. However, my dad was more often out helping others than spending time with me. We had different interests, but we both shared a genuine spiritual connection. Some of my best memories are of playing my viola during church services just before he preached, visiting nursing homes with him, playing my viola for the services, and spending lots of time with him and my family in nature at our beloved cabin in northern Minnesota.

When the sting of losing my dad first hit me, I felt a great sense of lack, which included painfully comparing my sibling's relationship with him. Then, during this meditation, when I felt the love that was beneath it all, I finally understood that nothing else mattered. I felt a huge sense of resolve, peace, and gratitude. This breakthrough cut straight through the old feelings of lack and unworthiness. It filled in my missing notes, as I became connected to that core string that connects us to everything.

As an adult, I had a good relationship with my dad. I mostly remember his brave fifteen-year battle with Parkinson's disease.

He remained positive, he never showed self-pity, he never complained, and he never lost an ounce of his strong faith. I never missed a chance to play hymns for him and my mom while he would sing along. When he had almost lost his voice, he would clap his hands to thank me. I will always remember the time I played for him at a care facility, as I stood near a cage of beautiful finches. During a pause, one of the birds clearly whistled the melody, as if heaven had orchestrated the notes.

I've also had a mostly good relationship with my mom now that I've grown up. Though she had her reasons not always to be positive, they are distant memories. Instead of dwelling on the past, I turned my attention toward healing the psychological imprint that still lingered. No longer would I unconsciously repeat damaging patterns caused by self-doubt and neediness, which only deepened my pain and fueled my search for approval.

I realized the negative subconscious patterns that were created when I was a child no longer served me. When I allowed my Higher Power to remove them, I was able to fill that space with my "missing notes." I understand that the healing journey can be a slow and steady process, requiring time, faith, and patience. Often, we think we've addressed and healed a negative core belief, only to have it show up later as yet another "missing note" in our lives. It can be frustrating and confusing and cause greater setbacks in our spiritual development than the actual problem we're facing. So, how do we deal with that issue and continue forward in the healing process without judgment about our progress?

I believe we come into this life with lessons we need to learn, but it's our choice whether we want to learn them or not. Some people might believe this is part of karma and there's no escaping it. But, I feel that our lessons come with major themes. These lessons will keep on showing up with deeper levels of meaning and importance until we address them and learn them. The volume is turned up each time we don't get the message, or only partially get it, so that we might hear it this time.

For instance, we'll hear a whisper, but might choose to ignore it. And, then the lesson will come in a regular voice, then a loud voice, and finally a shouting, screaming voice until the message is received. We could have been spared so much heartache if we'd been in tune with the signals that the universe sent back when the message first came as a whisper. Intuition, which is God's voice, is usually very soft, and we need to listen closely to hear it.

When our lessons come back to us time and again, we must remember that it isn't about any one incident. It's about coming to terms with significant life themes. We will be "tested "with different versions of these themes, especially based on how well we're listening. There's a story about a Catholic Saint, who, when faced with the pain of a returning negative event, resisted the urge to dwell on disappointment, judgment, or upset. Instead, the saint replied, "Welcome little friend; it's you again," and continued with what she was doing without disruption. When you can practice this kind of surrender and acceptance, you will notice how much faster you can hear the still, small voice and respond effectively.

Meditation and prayer are two of the most effective ways to increase our ability to hear the voice of God speaking in our lives. As you enter into your daily personal prayer time or whatever practice of meditation is most comfortable, ask for guidance and gifts from a Higher Power to direct your awareness to the places within that still need healing, to the places that feel damaged or incomplete. And, make the time, space, and silence, to hear the answers. Ask to be shown, through insight and revelation, what changes need to be made to fill those missing notes with new harmonies and new life. Then, trust, let go, and believe that welcoming the higher vibrations are shifting the disharmony to harmony and that what is out of alignment is being perfectly adjusted.

I use a listening meditation to help this process along. To practice this meditation, get comfortable, close your eyes, and take a big breath in through your nose. Hold the breath and release the air through your mouth. Repeat this a few times and then breathe normally. You can feel the vibrations made when the air fills your nostrils and then when the air passes through your lips. Now, focus on the sounds around you—a ticking clock, the refrigerator, a plane flying overhead, or the traffic outside. Focus on the sounds and feel "held" by the sounds for as long as possible. Feel the vibrations from these sounds and let them fill every part of you, including the negative "holes" inside. Feel the vibrations as gifts from the universe filling you with love.

To fill in the missing notes, we must first clear the blocks. SoundPath provides many different ways to release the subconscious negative programs. Drums and percussion instruments are invaluable tools on our SoundPath journey. You might be wondering how this will help you when you aren't a drummer, and you don't own any drums. We are born as a rhythm machine: the heart beats rhythmically, pumping blood through the veins into the heart as it beats and pushes our life-giving force through our internal network of veins. We have breathing rhythms and patterns, we have biological rhythms, and electrical activity in the brain.

We can find drums and percussion sound-makers all around us when we start looking. A pencil and small plastic container make a little drum, an empty round oatmeal container, and a wooden spoon work well too. A larger bucket with two spoons can create lots of beats. Pull out some of your metal lids and find the ones with the best sound when you strike the different parts of it and try different wooden spoons. It's easy to put some rice or beans in a small container; closing it up with tape, makes for a great shaker or rattle. If no such tools are available, how about your steering wheel when you are sitting at a red light or stalled in traffic? One of the best drums is you! You are the drum and the drummer when you learn to do body percussion. Try it!

Releasing stuck emotions is very good for our physical and emotional health. Next time something is bothering you, see it as an opportunity to release blocks and bring in the joy you have been missing. Find a piece of paper and a pen and whatever drum you have created, official drums are also allowed. Fold the paper in half vertically. Think of your issue; on the left side, write what is out-of-tune and upsetting. On the right side, list things that are going well, where you can feel harmony and gratitude. Now, feel the difference in the vibrational level and choose which side you want to release. Now, tear up the paper, pause, think about your feelings about the list, and play it on your drum as you release it. Look at the list on the right side and play an affirming rhythm expressing your gratitude and what you want more of in your life.

The gong has a powerful effect and can help you to raise your vibrational level. As Li Shangyin wrote in 813-858 AD, "if we trust the true and sure words written in the Indian leaves, we will hear all past and future in one stroke of the temple bell." I suggest that you find a wooden spoon and a metal lid from your kitchen; a metal Bundt pan is my favorite. You don't make a direct hit that would scatter energy, but instead, you make a downward or upward stroke with grace as the energy is directed.

Playing the gong with positive intention represents how to play and approach your actions and attitudes in your life.

The pure sound waves of a gong penetrate the body and mind. They clear the subconscious mind, elevating your vibration, and restoring harmony and vitality. You can't keep a negative thought; it must be released, while positive thoughts are reinforced. You only need to relax into the sound—the vibration will do the work. It's like experiencing a sonic massage! You will feel refreshed, in tune, and aligned with a clear, uplifted vibration.

Yogi Bhajan, Ph.D., wrote that a gong will "repair the nervous system and create deep relaxation. It releases you from the torrent of thoughts and stimulates the glandular system to a higher level of functioning."

The goal of SoundPath is to help you reach higher levels of vibration, functioning, and joy in your life. I once gave a few sessions to a client who faced many struggles. She grew up in a large family with very few of her basic needs met. She suffered from sexual abuse as a child and needed to care for her needs from a very early age. As an adult, she struggled with her relationships with men. They were abusive, and several had drug problems. She had a reasonably successful career but had difficulty spending within her means. We worked on releasing the negative subconscious programming that was etched deep into her cells and habits. She intently wanted help to find a supportive partner, someone to be with her and treat her well. Certainly, after all of her years of struggles, this shouldn't have been too much to ask.

As healing comes in layers, many layers of programming needed clearing. She was able to make some good progress, and things began to turn around. However, her constant devaluing experience with others caused her to mainly focus on herself, in narcissistic ways, interfering with her ability to attract what she desired. I remember one session that presented an example of her "missing notes." She had recently been treated horribly by her grandson, who was a young teenager. Of course, it is important to learn how to put up boundaries and not allow yourself to be poorly treated, with no appreciation or respect. We worked on releasing negative subconscious programs. Toward the end of the session, she mentioned, in passing, that her grandson had attempted to commit suicide earlier in the week. She was most concerned about how his pain had affected her while she basically didn't consider the cause beneath his behavior, or her grandson's loud call for help. I am familiar with these dynamics; my heart felt a lot of compassion, and my prayers were sent for the grandson's suffering and also for her, as his grandma, who was reliving unresolved negative programming and patterns.

This story illustrates the truth that when we are running negative subconscious programs, we are the only ones that can't see them. I know that God has more than enough love for all of us. Some people who have more missing notes will have a longer road to travel before their negative subconscious patterns become quieter and less than the positive patterns and messages of unconditional love.

These are but a few of the tools and exercises—more will follow—that can help fill the holes and replace your missing notes. You can use them at any time to raise your vibration until you no longer resonate with what you believe is wrong or incomplete about you. The higher vibrations will re-pattern those pathways, proving new insights about who you are, what you're capable of accomplishing, and what you deserve to experience in your relationship with others. But, it takes an alertness to changing circumstances and an awareness to know when you start shifting into the default settings. New tools can allow us to reprogram the software and to use these new patterns that are filled with love, joy, respect, and growth.

Sometimes, it can be difficult to make these adjustments in real time, especially, when we're faced with circumstances that have regularly triggered us in the past. But, one technique that I've found to be of great help is to think of something that might alert you like a "red flag." It can be something as simple as snapping a bracelet, or taking a deep breath, and using those vibrations to shift your mindset when faced with the old feelings and thought patterns. Any cue you can think of to disrupt, or block the default setting before it takes root will eventually start to dislocate the negative patterns in advance. This will prevent them from starting the downward spiral of negativity that destroys the harmony and overpowers the new melodies you're trying to create.

I turn to these exercises to feel relief from a painful old pattern before it takes hold of me. After I have finished a big performance, for instance, I may start to notice any and all ways it wasn't perfect. The scorching internal pain, shame, embarrassment can be like embers; if given extra air and fuel, a full blazing fire could erupt. In the past, I would loop the critic's review along with the review committee in my mind, you know those non-stop critical voices, right? and be wrought with self-critical thoughts. Now, because I have changed much of my subconscious programming, I can recognize this pattern in the beginning, and I apply the tools as I choose and rehearse the kinder, gentler, and loving pathway.

Today, I have found freedom and joy performing my viola as I have applied these concepts, which I am now presenting as part of SoundPath. As my subconscious beliefs were re-programmed and replaced with faith and trust instead of fear and judgment, the experience and my results have been transformed. I rely heavily on my improvisational skills, which require me to release the control of my mind as I go up and connect with God. I need to have one hundred percent faith and intensely focused listening, which can also be called "channeling," as my intention is to be a channel of God's love, streaming through my heart to the listener's heart. If fear were to peek in for even a second, the flow would stop immediately. Faith and fear cannot co-exist.

One of my breakthroughs came when I successfully uncovered a subconscious pattern of being afraid of making a mistake, not being perfect, not a good enough musician and performer. The key to my breakthrough was to take on the belief that there are no wrong notes! I'm improvising, and whatever note I play is the perfect one! I feel such great joy when I allow this process to happen freely in a performance or life. Then, I can see the results on the listener's faces, including tears and radiant joy, and hear stories of the positive changes they feel.

The process of recording my eight CDs has also been filled with many gifts of inspiration and joy. The worst critics, headed up by myself, have needed to go into retirement or find other jobs—they are no longer employed!

Sound and vibrations are whole and complete. Through these exercises, we can allow the sound to fill up those places of lack. Listen with openness, acceptance, and love.

The shape of a sound wave can be turned and overlapped and seen as an infinity symbol. The overlapping point in the center of the infinity symbol is our place of stillness and wholeness connecting with God. This point also represents the past, present, and future, connected in the moment we are in. The still point is our timeless moment of connecting to God.

It is in this still center that we can connect to our core vibrating string that links us to God, creation, ourselves, and everyone else. From this place, it's very easy to see that there has never been anything missing from you—or the beautifully orchestrated symphony that is your life.

SoulString Alignment Exercise

Remember that our breath is a valuable instrumental tool always with us, offering vibration, rhythm, and life. Get comfortable. Notice how you are feeling now. Take a deep breath from your stomach, allow it to expand. Feel the air vibrate your lips as you release the air through your mouth.

Take another breath and envision the vibrations rising up and connecting you to the heavens. As you exhale, let go of any pain. Breathe in again and feel peace, white light and love.

Now exhale, feel the energy travel through your body, your feet, and into the core of the earth, as any final dissonance is released. Feel yourself grounded.

Repeat. Experience it.

Expand your energy and feel it move through your aura, the space that surrounds you. Ask a Higher Power to give you a symbol of protection and place it on the front edge of your aura. The symbol may be a color or a feeling of knowing that you are surrounded by and connected with Universal Energy and truth.

Let your awareness return to your breath moving up and connecting to the highest source of Universal energy, the energy of All that Is. Release, ground, and connect to the earth. Feel the vibrations of your breath as a vibrating string connecting you to the heavens above and deep inside the core of the earth. This vibrating string clears and aligns you and dissonance is resolved.

You are balanced, connected to your truth, peaceful, powerful, and in harmony.

Notice how you are feeling now. This is SoulString Alignment.

Do this exercise as often as needed, remembering that the transformational benefits always offer relief that is only a breath away.

TWO

VIBRATION

Our universe exists as an all-encompassing field of vibrational energy. These energetic waves, tones, and vibrations, converge to create universal harmony—a mathematically precise, unfathomably perfect symphony that, though inaudible to the human ear, orchestrates the quality of life on Earth and throughout the cosmos. Poets and scientists have long referred to these vibrational tones as "the music of the spheres." No matter what we call them, the resulting harmony has the power to bring about benefits that go far beyond what our human efforts could ever dictate.

Albert Einstein once said, "Everything in life is vibration." This includes us. Our bodies pulsate at a particular vibration, also called a frequency. But, what does this mean? Think of a radio signal. You cannot see a frequency being emitted. But, when you tune to your favorite radio station, the results are quite evident!

Consider the brain. You are probably familiar with the fact that it operates at various frequencies, depending on its function at the time. When you are sleeping, the brain operates in the "delta" state, between 0.1 and 3 hertz (Hz). When you are meditating, your brain tends to rest in the "theta" state of 4 to 7 Hz. The "alpha' state is from 8 to 14 Hz. In the "beta" state, the brain's vibration speeds up to between 15 and 40 Hz. The other organs in the body pulse or vibrate at their own distinct levels.

And, there are other, largely invisible energetic activities in the body that contribute to one's unique frequency or vibration.

Our bodies vibrate on a cellular level, and the vibration continues out beyond the body in a vibratory continuum. The vibration you emit is reflected back. If your vibration is one of anger, depression, or sadness, you emit that into the space around you. And, it can be reflected back to you. This is important. If you can raise your frequency or vibration, you can attract experiences that create more positive opportunities in life.

Our thoughts, feelings, words, and actions also resonate at specific vibrational frequencies that are either in harmony or out of harmony with the greater universal flow. Our minds and bodies respond instantly to corresponding vibrations, literally bypassing the conscious mind. Thus, it's possible to use vibrations in a purposeful effort to connect directly to the universal force that links our minds, bodies, and spirits, while balancing our emotions in the process.

The key is in the subconscious mind and our emotions, which have the potential to influence the make-up of every cell of our bodies. The subconscious is the part of the mind that operates below the level of our conscious awareness. Think of an iceberg. The conscious mind is the part we can see above the water. It has a wide variety of tasks and responsibilities, from regulating breathing to making sense of the world. The subconscious is that enormous mass of ice beneath. It picks up subtle clues from others; it notices when something isn't "right." It is the source of intuition. It creates emotions. The root causes of many emotional and physical problems reside in the subconscious mind.

So, why do our minds and bodies respond instantly to vibration both sub-consciously and emotionally? Because vibration is the universal "language" we speak, through which our minds and bodies function at the most elemental levels.

Think of it like this: if your boss shouted and screamed at you in Korean, but you only knew how to speak English, you would not understand anything that was said. Certain messages would come through—however, not what your boss wanted you to understand. Most likely you would interpret the message in descriptive terms, such as "good" or "bad" or "urgent" or "do this" (whatever the "this" is that you do not completely understand). Very quickly these messages would affect your attitude toward your boss probably negatively and even toward yourself. But, if you began to learn Korean, you would begin to hear the message accurately, with less agitation and misinterpretation.

This same concept applies to your ability to learn subliminally from vibrations. You can begin to feel and understand the messages you are already being sent by those around you and indeed by the universe itself. Vibrations also can allow us to speak directly and effectively to our bodies and even the subconscious mind—the level from which almost every decision is made and acted upon.

Unfortunately, we've been led to believe that we can communicate with others and control our environment solely through conscious effort. We believe that the only way to change our lives is to harness the power of the conscious mind. Of course, we do have the ability to use discipline and willpower to accomplish goals and shape our lives in a positive way. We also can make an effort to communicate with others effectively. And, with enough effort, change will occur, at least for a while.

But, without changing our subconscious programming—our core beliefs—we'll eventually run into the same pitfalls, repeating mental or emotional patterns over and over, even when the conscious mind is shouting, "But, you know better!" This is why reprogramming our core beliefs—shaped in early childhood until the age of seven—is crucial to better our lives.

In the first seven years of a person's life, the natural maturing process of the human species involves gathering information by observation and forming a bass level of subconscious awareness and processing methodology. Until the age of seven, we are learning about the world and who we are by the observations we make and the experiences we have. To use a computer analogy, during the first seven years of our lives, our brains are loaded with an operating system that is rarely updated after we leave childhood. An operating system in a computer works best, if at all, only with the correct processors, which must interpret the electrical signals and send them where they are understood. Our brains work the same way. After the age of seven, the programming has been "hard-wired" into who we are, and we attract experiences based on these programs.

These core beliefs shape not only who we are but they most likely are the very ones that our parents learned before they were seven years old.

Thanks to the work of forward-thinking scientists like Bruce Lipton, we know now that our genes do not determine our fate; they serve as a blueprint that receives information from our core beliefs. In other words, our programming controls our genes.

But, our brains, like computers, can be improved. It may seem impossible, but SoundPath, backed by science and experience, has demonstrated that we can use vibrations, the fundamental element of universal energy, to "tune" our bodies and minds like we tune instruments. We can train ourselves to play in masterful harmony with our conscious desires, allowing them to grow, develop, and unfold with relative ease, by opening new pathways in the brain into the subconscious mind, whose patterns have for the most part been shut off from revision since the age of seven.

What if we could reach the recesses of our subconscious minds with the right effort and methodology? What if we could reprogram portions of our subconscious minds, long after the age of seven, and replace the old "wiring" in our minds with new pathways that we can program from our perspective as free-thinking adults? We'd then have a powerful technique for communicating with ourselves and others, both consciously and subconsciously. We'd be more in alignment with the energy of the universe, which is capable of healing emotional trauma, physical pain, and illness. We'd become capable of realizing our most heartfelt desires for success and self-development, while finally learning how to bypass the pitfalls that keep us stuck in the same old ruts.

If this sounds too good to be true, I assure you it is not. Open your eyes to the world around you. Within your lifetime, you have seen some people experience what may seem to be a "charmed life," filled with whatever their hearts desired maybe things you have desired, but have not achieved. Some people call that just dumb luck. But, it is not.

String theory of quantum physics, the "Theory of Everything", posits that the universe, and all matter, is comprised entirely of vibrating strings of energy. String theory proposes that at the deepest invisible level of matter, everything, from the giant stars and planets to the smallest particles, is made up of minuscule elastic strands—or strings—of energy. The difference in the particle of matter that is created relates to the resonant pitch at which the string vibrates.

According to string theory, the human body can be seen as symphonic strings, vibrating inside of us, as well as, resonating with our external environment. However, this isn't a new phenomenon, since the knowledge that vibration, energy, and sound, can improve our health has been around for more than five thousand years. Hermetic philosophers believed that vibration was one of the seven major principles on which life is based. Everything is in motion, and everything vibrates. Chinese healers, including acupuncturists today, aim to restore energy flow, or *chi*, by opening and balancing the meridians. Pythagoras taught the "music of spheres" – that movement, rhythm, and the vibration of every atom and celestial body creates a unique and particular sound. Based on this understanding, he used music to heal the body and emotions.

These theories demonstrate how sound can change substance. Because we're all connected, strand by strand, to the harmonizing power of the universe, our thoughts create energy that taps into and triggers a similar energy in physical matter. Ernst Chladni, a pioneer of experimental acoustics, demonstrated this in simple visual experiments. In one such experiment, Chladni drew a violin bow along the edge of a plate covered with fine sand. The sand formed various geometric patterns according to the sound the bow produced. His achievement in relating sound and waves paved the way for the acoustical theory of waves.

Have you ever asked yourself what sound a blossoming flower might make? Would the sound change depending on the color? Quite possibly, thought a Swiss physician and scientist named Dr. Hans Jenny, who desired to "hear" the systems of nature. In *Cymatics: A Study of Wave Phenomena and Vibration*, Jenny describes his experiments placing sand, powders, and liquids on steel plates, which he vibrated using a frequency generator with crystal transducers attached to the plates. His experiments produced beautiful and intricate patterns that were unique to each individual vibration. (See photos below).

1. Lycopodium powder spread on a steel plate

2. Same plate except the pitch/frequency is raised

3. Bach, Toccata, and Fugue m.30 before Andante

4. Mozart, Jupiter Symphony 1st Mvt. M. 173, beat 3

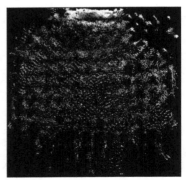

These patterns remained intact as long as the sound pulsed through the substance. When the sound stopped, the pattern collapsed. Jenny loved to study nature's cycle of the seasons—a bird's feathers, a rain drop, the formation of weather patterns, mountains, or ocean waves—even poetry, the periodic table of elements, or music. In all of these things, Jenny saw an underlying, unifying theme: wave patterns produced by vibration. Jenny saw everything in terms of "periodicities and rhythmicities." He believed that nature is created using this periodic style reflected in patterns of vibration.

Learning about these amazing discoveries led me to wonder: if sound can change substances, what can it alter inside of us? What role could sound play in creating and sustaining the cells of our own bodies? There's been ample evidence, across various cultures and disciplines, that vibration and sound can interact with our molecules and stimulate healing. How, then, do the vibrational patterns of a diseased body differ from the patterns the body emanates when it's healthy? How can we turn the unhealthy vibrations into healthy ones? What specific kinds of vibrations resonate with health and wellness? How can we use sound to create peace in our mind and wellness in our body? How can we hear our guiding messages and tap into the subconscious patterns that rule us?

As it turns out, symmetrical patterns in music offer some incredibly beneficial effects for listeners. In music, using symmetrical, or repetitive, patterns can be called a motif, or if used longer, it is called an ostinato. If it is part of the larger form, it is called recapitulation, as in the ABA form when the A section repeats. Repetition makes the listener feel safe when what is known returns. Bach, Mozart, Beethoven, and other classically trained composers practiced this symmetry of pattern and repetition in their music while masterfully weaving in elements of surprise, which continues to delight and enrapt listeners to this day. Music from the Baroque and Classical periods uses diatonic harmonies. These harmonies follow a strict pattern of rules about what chord can follow and what direction each note of a chord must go, up or down, as it finds the resolution, or movement, to the next note.

This also is the pattern used in Western culture's nursery rhymes, folk songs, hymns, and much of today's popular music. We're wired, from our ears to our nervous system, to internalize these predictable patterns, which I believe provides a sense of safety and calm. When overtones are vibrating together, these patterns create an openness and beauty in the sound.

When several sounds come together to make a note, it may be called an overtone. This is, of course, a simplification of the concept. For those of you more musically inclined, consider this: an overtone is one of an ascending series of mostly imperceptible sonic components that sound above a clearly audible fundamental pitch. In other words, a certain "sounding" note includes a number of higher frequencies making up the harmonic spectrum of the sound that combine to form the sound we are "hearing." The pitch we "hear" is called the fundamental. If this seems too technical, just know that a note needs to sound pure and be in tune to activate the overtones fully. This is what creates a full, beautiful ringing note.

However, when there's dissonance, which means that the notes are clashing together, somewhat similar to the sound of traffic or a loud horn honking, we beg for it to stop. Dissonance has a predictable pattern of moving to the next chord that is "resonant." The dissonance kind of loosens up the sounds that don't fit and requires them to shift into position.

In an aligned state, the body instinctively seeks out balance, wholeness, and wellness. When we're misaligned, dissonance can be experienced in many different ways, such as physical illness or emotional instability. Dissonance resonates with anger. It's like the emotional equivalent of heavy metal music or any genre of music where the chaos of the sound is created with force, almost like a rhythmic pounding of frustrations. Notes clash, each one fighting to be heard like a shouting match between two people. It represents confused, unresolved energy. Dissonant energy is also closely related to the ego and its stubborn need to be right and in control.

Let's consider how dissonant energy affects us in our lives.

In the world of energy, to stay in dissonance brings oneself into isolation, prolonged misery, and increasing anger. To let go of the dissonance and anger means embracing the resolution that will bring peace. The person that we've been angry with can also experience the relief as well. When we are in a state of harmony, we can freely give and receive gifts, as we grow and our world grows.

The dissonance associated with sadness has a softer energy, an anguish that stems from a deep place in the soul. In feeling, hearing, and experiencing this kind of dissonance, we have the opportunity to acknowledge our humanness. We know, that, beneath it all, we can rest in the understanding that peace and resolution will come once we're ready to let it in.

Disease occurs when the dissonance and anguish in the mind become too much energy to contain, so it needs to release the chaos somewhere else. The body finds the weakest organ, and the chaos is released in the physical chemistry of the organ. People often report that "something felt off" or not quite right for quite a while before receiving a negative diagnosis. What if early dissonance could motivate a person to stop, listen, and make changes? Many of us wait until even more unbalance occurs in the body, and the symptoms grow louder—loud enough so that we're forced to stop, make changes, and seek treatment.

The SoundPath techniques can help to make any necessary health treatments easier, replacing anxiety and fear with peace and helping to align the body, so it is in its optimal state to accept treatment and return to wholeness and health. These techniques may be used continually to maintain the body, mind, and spirit balance and create new pathways so that the old patterns don't invite the dis-ease to return. Of course, and this is important, the suggestions presented here are meant to complement and enhance traditional treatments.

It has been said that my instrument, the viola, has a more favorable resonance of the overtones than other instruments, which would explain the richness, warmth, and the heightened ability to make subtle nuances of expression. One way in which overtones can be visibly demonstrated is by playing, for instance, the "C" note on the lowest string. If I place my finger very lightly on the string with my finger, not pressed down as it usually does to create a pitch, a "C" one octave higher is heard. An octave is the same essential note but at a different level. If I divide the string in half again, a fifth, an octave higher is heard, and there is a whole series. Our minds, bodies, and emotions respond to vibrational stimuli in the world in the same way that my viola responds to the notes that I play.

Everything—from different organs inside us, a room including concert halls, a drinking glass, to disease—have a resonant pitch, a note that acts like a microphone and invites all the overtones to ring together "in tune."

Even physical objects have a resonant pitch. This is how a singer can break a glass with her high note. When she sings a pure pitch that is the resonant pitch of the glass, the energy in the glass can't contain the added energy of the note joining it, so it breaks. The same thing happens when ultrasound finds the resonant pitch of a kidney stone, causing it to explode and shatter.

To take care of ourselves on every level, we need to recognize first how dissonant vibrations and tones affect us and then resolve them to create new vibrations of harmony. Unfortunately, the idea that vibration can affect physical matter isn't well understood by most people, though we live with the proof of it every day.

Researchers have created visual evidence of the power of sound to impact healing. In one experiment, noted French composer, acupuncturist, and sound healer, Fabien Maman, and biologist, Helene Grimal, experimented with both healthy and cancerous cells to see how they would respond to the voice and various instruments. In his book, *The Role of Music in the Twenty-First Century*, Maman demonstrated the progressive destabilization of the structure of cancer cells. Mounting a camera on a microscope with slides of human uterine cancer cells, Maman says that when he played sounds that progressed up the musical scale, the cancer cells exploded within minutes.

Japanese scientist Dr. Masaru Emoto has shown the potent effects of sound by photographing water crystals in a series of books, including *The Hidden Messages in Water*. His work was featured in the movie, "What the Bleep Do We Know?" In his remarkable experiments, he played classical music and folk songs through speakers placed next to water samples. He then froze the water to make crystals and compared the crystalline structure of the different samples. With each musical piece, the water sample formed different and beautifully geometric crystals. When he played heavy metal music, the water crystal's basic hexagonal structure broke into pieces.

Dr. Emoto also measured the impact of words on the crystalline structure of water. The results of his experiments demonstrated what spiritual masters have been teaching for centuries—that the words we speak and the thoughts we think impact our well-being and life on all levels. In one experiment, Dr. Emoto and three hundred others assembled at the shore of a badly polluted lake in Japan and spoke aloud an affirmation of peace and gratitude. The water crystals changed from a cloudy and distorted image before the prayer to beautiful, geometric crystals after the prayer. In another experiment, Dr. Emoto taped various words and phrases to jars of water. Afterward, he photographed the crystals formed when these water samples were frozen. Words or phrases such as "thank you," "love," and "peace" produced a variety of beautiful geometric forms. On the other hand, phrases such as "you make me sick" or "you fool" produced crystals that appeared disconnected or chaotic.

The implications of these simple experiments are profound. Since our bodies are made up of 70 percent water, imagine how the sounds and vibrations that fill our external environment affect our internal environment, even our very cells. Imagine how the words we speak about ourselves and others affect our health and the health and well-being of others.

This also is another example of string theory, the "Theory of Everything." We are one with all that is; we adjust to what's around us, resonating with the people we're connected to and with our core beliefs, whether positive or negative. In other words, we vibrate in sympathy with things around us that also maintain a similar frequency.

When we have sympathy for someone else, we can relate to what they're feeling. We often think of it in terms of "feeling someone else's pain." On a deeper level, as string theory suggests, we're all made up of the same core material or vibrating strings. So, as we change, we can affect change in someone else. This principle is demonstrated by the strings on a musical instrument that vibrate "in sympathy" with a pitch that it's related to. One activates the other, and they vibrate together. Also, when a string is played, a series of overtones vibrate with it, creating a complete, full, rich, clear sound.

In *The Biology of Belief*, Dr. Bruce Lipton discusses how Einstein's theory of relativity can explain what happens with the world on a large scale, and quantum theory explains the world on a very small scale but the two don't work together. Furthermore, these theories can't explain paranormal experiences like spontaneous healings or how the moving of chi reduces pain.

Dr. Lipton's book describes how new research in quantum physics, has established that matter is made up of spinning and vibrating energy. It is both a solid particle and an impenetrable force field. As is summarized by Dr. Lipton, "when the same atoms are described in terms of voltage potentials and wavelengths, they exhibit the qualities and properties of energy (waves)."

At the beginning of the twentieth century, physicists began researching the relationship between energy and matter. The new research, quantum physics, replaced the belief that matter is suspended in space, finding instead that matter is made up of spinning and vibrating energy. It is both a solid particle and an immaterial force field. Every form of matter, including humans, has a unique "energy signature." This is how scientists first discovered that vibrational frequencies are foundational. It's also why the soprano's voice can shatter glass and ultrasonic surgery works to break up kidney stones. When you want to break up an atom, you identify the appropriate frequency and tune a laser (or voice, as the case may be) to the right energy signature, and the atom is destroyed.

The messages of our energetic signatures are revealed through complex rhythms, which create the patterns that we see manifested throughout the natural world. A phenomenon called *entrainment*, when a more powerful frequency causes a weaker frequency to synchronize with it, explains how this occurs, and how rhythms persist even in the absence of environmental causes. The rhythms and patterns that are created don't exist due to any *learned* behavior. They are inherently entrained within an organism. One classic example is when several cuckoo clocks are placed on the same wall; within a matter of days, the pendulums all start swinging together. Entrainment explains how a flock of birds flying together can change direction at the same time.

Entrainment demonstrates how connected we are to those around us and our environment as well as how our energy level affects others. We do not exist in a vacuum. Awareness helps us to see choices and resources to make a huge difference in our own lives and those around us, near and far.

These concepts can sound esoteric and unrelated to our everyday lives at first glance. But, understanding the science and the mystery behind phenomena like sympathetic vibration, harmony, and entrainment, can change every aspect of our lives and provide the regular tune-ups our minds and bodies need for optimal living.

In the same way that a musician would tune an instrument, we can use sound vibrations to align our bodies for health. We can find the delicate balance that will neutralize negative core beliefs while allowing the body to heal and the mind to become clear. We can use sound, when properly understood and implemented, to literally cut new pathways through our subconscious blocks. When life deals us unwelcome surprises, or we face the inevitable tragedies that arise, we have tools at our disposal that can quickly and effectively bring us back into harmony.

The first step in learning how to do this is to practice awareness. This means taking the time to stop and listen and feel the dissonance when it arises. But, recognizing dissonance within ourselves is trickier than it appears. We often don't even notice or realize the level of pain, anger, and disharmony we experience on a regular basis. After a while, the average person acclimates to the ongoing pains of their life. We may vaguely know that we'd like to change. Other people's lives may seem much better than ours, making us feel sad or wistful or envious. We may believe that a lot of people have things better and easier than us. We may even feel very sorry for ourselves, caught in a cycle of victimhood—which is a cycle I know very well. But, none of these thoughts or feelings equate to the type of awareness that can bring about true healing. We don't need to imagine what is going on inside someone else's life, especially, when we can keep very busy creating the life we want.

When a person has been stuck for so long, it can become difficult even to imagine how good life can be. It's part of the human condition to get used to functioning at whatever level one has become accustomed to—whether it's healthy or not. For example, if you subtly and gradually get sick, it may take an acute downturn before you finally start to think, *Wow, I need to do something. I feel terrible.*

But, it doesn't have to be this way. We just need to develop the awareness, and the means to hit the pause button.

The following exercise helps me to shift to a better place. It is an exceptionally effective practice to do this as you are falling asleep and waking up when your brain is passing through the theta state.

Sit comfortably, close your eyes, focus on your breath. Take a deep breath in, feel the vibrations as the air passes through your nose. Let your stomach expand as the air travels into your lungs, hold your breath, then release through your mouth as you feel the air vibrate your lips. Take another deep, clearing breath of life, hold, and then release everything that isn't helpful. Repeat a few more times and then breathe comfortably.

Focus on the sounds around you, every little sound. Feel the sounds vibrate inside of you, continue to feel yourself in the middle of the sounds, in the middle of your music, in the middle of your life connected to all that is.

Feel yourself held by the sounds. Continue to listen to the sounds that you usually block out. Let them bring you peace. As you connect to the vibrations of the sounds around you, let the sounds vibrate within you. Feel connected, feel one with the vibrations everywhere. Give gratitude for the gifts of sound, vibration, and life.

The sounds are outside of yourself, all around you, yet also within when you invite them in. Focusing on the sounds takes the attention away from your thoughts and analytical conscious mind chatter so that you can experience stillness and clarity. This meditation becomes a peaceful distraction that helps you to shift from dissonance into harmony.

The first step in raising your emotional vibrational level is to become aware of what level you're at. Dr. David R. Hawkins, renowned author, scientist, and expert in the fields of consciousness research and spirituality created a way to represent the levels of consciousness on a numerical scale. He assigned different moods and feelings a number, which he demonstrated on a pyramid. If we identify a low vibrational level, we can acknowledge it, process the negative emotions that would otherwise keep us stuck, and then move to a higher level.

But, this process can be extremely difficult when you don't have the right tools. I think most of us can relate to the experience of having something terrible happen, and the first thing that we do is call up someone else who can commiserate with us. While it may feel helpful in a moment to vent our problems and issues, and it is important to feel and express the anger and be upset. However, it doesn't help us to stay in that place. Ultimately, we're magnifying and reinforcing the pain. Sharing our heartbreaks and disappointments with those closest to us is a normal and natural impulse, but we must keep in mind that the ultimate goal is to express it, release it, and then choose to move on. I'm not suggesting that you force yourself to move on before being ready. But, it will be impossible to raise your vibration if you get stuck in the story and choose to "live there." We can observe what subconscious programs are running and choose ways to release them and replace them with healthy, positive habits.

I once traveled to a retirement facility to teach a program that included drumming. One woman was younger than the other participants, but her posture reflected that of a much older woman. She was bent over in a wheelchair, and her hands were curled. For her to participate in the drumming, I needed to adapt the mallet. Even with that accommodation, she wasn't able to participate very much.

It was near St. Patrick's Day, and I played an Irish jig. One of the chefs who had been preparing lunch, heard the music, lept out from the kitchen and began step dancing. He demonstrated his great skill with a whole lot of joy. Before long, this woman jumped out of her wheelchair and began dancing with him! I will never forget seeing her face filled with joy that radiated throughout her being. I felt present to a miracle, privileged to witness her instantaneously tap into a higher source of energy, a greater level of vibration and energy.

Another time, I was giving ten-minute sound healing sessions at an expo and I worked with a woman who had experienced a stroke. She couldn't smile because her lips were frozen, and she couldn't move her mouth on one side of her face, which affected her speech. Nevertheless, she began to share with me the rape and abuse that she'd experienced as a child. She said that she had never told anyone about it. Our music and energy work enabled her to release the negative energy and pain she had held in her body for so many years. Her face began to relax, and the paralysis disappeared! She left that day wearing the biggest smile and talked with ease.

Time and again, I've experienced incredible healings and had miracles take place when people were able to raise their vibrations. In the book *Molecules of Emotion*, author Candice Pert explains that when we feel an emotion, our bodies react, creating neuropeptides that pass through the bloodstream into receptors in the brain and throughout the body. Neurotransmitters like serotonin, along with other endorphins, are released. Pert writes, "Our emotions and other people's emotions affect our bodies, and so do our personal beliefs—and the beliefs of those around us that we've come to internalize."

Considering the connection between our body, mind, and spirit, we can see how important it is to pay attention to our feelings, how we deal with them, and how we connect to those around us. Learning to communicate with our subconscious beliefs and re-pattern our negative habits allows us to find ways to put our bodies back in balance. And, when we can do that for ourselves, it becomes that much easier to do it in our relationships with other people.

SoundPath focuses on how we can change our thoughts by communicating with and reprogramming our subconscious core beliefs so that our thoughts can change, which will then change not only our physical body but our mind, spirit, and lives as well.

By applying the SoundPath techniques, you'll learn how to consciously take the steps necessary to stabilize, find harmony, and raise your vibration whenever you're faced with the inevitable upsets life brings. Rather than living with mental and emotional blocks and a weakened physical condition that otherwise could lead to disease, we'll work on innovative ways to reclaim our power. Healthy communication is one of the emotional components we will focus on since it is key to dealing with so many of our underlying issues.

The necessity of choosing a new SoundPath was brought home for me when I was diagnosed with bilateral breast cancer two years ago. It was immediately clear to me that I needed to make major changes in my life. I'd read and heard many stories about how a person's attitude about life and death directly determined their lifespan. So, for me, the choices I needed to make weren't about chemotherapy or tamoxifen or surgery, which were the treatment options I was given. My choice was whether I was willing to go deeper in my practice, raise my vibration, and uncover yet another, deeper layer of healing that needed to be addressed. Of course, I also had surgery while I was engaged in my inner work. I don't mean to suggest for a second that anyone should not listen to and follow medical advice. But, my greatest lesson was that my cancer diagnosis urged me to examine how I allowed myself to be treated by others, especially those closest to me, and this included myself.

For years, I'd accepted the role of always doing for others, being invisible, and not receiving respect for my gifts and passions. As a consequence, I experienced dissonance in different areas of my life. More than anything, I wanted to heal. So, my choice was clear. I used the SoundPath techniques to raise my vibration, adjust my outlook, and it gave my entire life the tune-up it needed. In fact, writing this book is a huge example of the changes that I have learned, made, and continue to make.

This is an exercise to integrate the concept of knowing that you are separate from your thoughts and circumstances and that you have choices. These choices will reinforce our brains' neuroplasticity, which creates miracles of change when we make the choice to change. We can learn to choose to stop a painful thought, create a detour from the ingrained pathway of pain, and create a new pathway of freedom, hope, and ease.

When a painful situation or an uncomfortable, judgmental thought arises: visualize yourself separate from the thought as you stand in an active stream and attempt to walk upstream against the current. The sound of the roaring water adds to the discomfort. Feel the struggle as hidden rocks scrape against you, it is cold and raining, the end isn't in sight, as you become increasingly tired. You are getting nowhere. This has been the only choice you thought you had.

Now, imagine that you are standing in a stream and you realize a new choice. As you start to walk with the current, there is a gentle warm breeze filled with the fragrance smell of flowers, the sun peeks in and out of the clouds, you hear the sound of rippling water, beautiful birds are flying and singing, butterflies flitter about, and you move forward with ease in that stream.

Imagine a difficult situation you have or are facing; allow yourself to choose to travel the well-worn pathway of pain or to make a different choice and create and reinforce a new pathway of support and ease. Create your image, including details of what you will experience along this new pathway. Ground this vision with special sounds on your drum while you repeat an affirmingn phrase, or mantra. Feel each step taken with ease and support, celebrating the freedom. Think of that special sound, maybe a drum or bell for instance, that can remind you to choose and follow the new pathway as soon as you've been triggered by a painful pattern. Now you have a choice to do something new as you travel your pathway to freedom.

Today, my life is completely transformed for the better. I am healthy, happy, and living a life that I love while helping others. My relationships have grown stronger, and I'm proud of the work I've done to change the unhealthy core beliefs that were holding me back. This type of reawakening is possible for anyone. It's a fundamental part of what I believe and want to share.

We have choices that give us great power now and in the future. Being in tune with our highest vibrations helps align us to our divine purpose. Cultivating vibrational attunement uncovers and removes negative blocks and helps to create new habits while it harmonizes our truth with all that is. As the dissonance is cleared, we can freely move forward on our path connected to divine peace and love.

THREE
It's All About the Bass

You may think of your beliefs as consciously held convictions. But, most beliefs are not in our conscious awareness. In fact, a belief is at the core of every decision, habit, and pattern in our lives. These are the subconscious core beliefs that create our reality.

Core beliefs are created before the age of seven, when a child doesn't know how to discern the truth about their experiences and what they're told. These beliefs tell us who we believe we are; what we are worthy of, including our self-worth; and, how we not only deserve, but "need" to be treated based on our "given" role in life. These beliefs include what we need physically, emotionally, and spiritually; the level of our abilities, our intelligence, appearance, body image, artistic, and athletic gifts; our social skills; what we "owe" others; our relationship with God, including what we believe God feels about us; what we deserve and "need" to do to be worthy—you get the idea. These impressions become part of our basic "computer programming," a central part of our underlying "operating system" that the subconscious mind automatically replays throughout life.

SoundPath helps access and change the negative subconscious beliefs, not to re-write them, but to re-wire the brain.

It is important to look at the themes of our first seven years, taking note of those that have impacted our subconscious minds.

In my case, I was born and raised in a rather strict, religious Scandinavian family in Minnesota. My mother was a dedicated English and special education teacher, and my father was a prominent Lutheran minister who started his church when I was five years old. My dad was an incredible man and a dedicated, effective, and charismatic leader. When he retired after thirty-five years, the modest church he founded had grown into a congregation of three thousand members, housed in a beautiful church building filled with incredible features, including a full-sized indoor basketball court.

People wrote tributes about how my dad saved their lives. At least a dozen people entered the ministry as a direct result of my dad's influence. He served our community tirelessly. He started a homeless shelter and after-school care before anyone had even heard of doing those things because he was committed to meeting the needs of others. My mother was extremely dedicated to her family, while tirelessly serving her role as the minister's wife of a large congregation and caring for her special education students. I'm very thankful for the mixture of faith, hard work, and commitment they showed me.

I am blessed to come from a long line of ministers. My dad handed down to me a coveted cross that has been in our family since it was owned by a Bishop of Norway in the 1800s. One uncle was a very dedicated missionary in the Philippines. Another was a Baptist minister. I know that deep-seeded faith was passed down to me, along with influences from my dad's commitment as a spiritual seeker. I loved going through his extensive library filled with an eclectic collection of psychology, world religions, the writings of spiritual giants, and many devotional books. Recently, during a break from writing, I pulled out one of his favorite devotional books. I opened it to a passage that spoke about humility: "Our merits and manners are like dead leaves before the wind—before we can be of use to God we must be broken, crushed, sometimes even to the point of despair." The verse it was based on was Luke 14:11, "For everyone who exalts himself will be humbled." This gave me added insights as to my upbringing and my conflicting beliefs about myself. I am so thankful I was given the gift to know God as a loving, non-judgmental God, who has unconditional love for everyone who asks. But, as a child, I also experienced mixed messages about my worthiness versus my "inherent sinful nature".

I remember a time when my mom and I visited my dad in the hospital after a surgery. The man in the bed next to him was dying. My dad wanted to serve him communion, so my mom brought his communion box. Even though his voice had been weakened by Parkinson's, his mind was sharp, and his intentions were strong. However, his mobility was limited because he was in a wheelchair. As he spoke and prayed, I was the one to reach over to the man and serve him the communion. I clearly remember—and I treasure—what it felt like to be an extension of my dad's arms and hands in service. I like to think I may be carrying on my dad's spiritual legacy and desire to serve others.

Our family culture prided itself on Scandinavian stoicism. I never knew what a Minnesota accent sounded like until I saw the movie *Fargo*. When I listened to Garrison Keillor's radio show, "A Prairie Home Companion," I was not one bit amused as he told all too familiar stories about my world. It hit home when he spoke about the church people, the Lutherans of Lake Wobegon. He loved to talk about the church's potluck staples, like molded Jell-O filled with canned fruit, and the variety of casseroles that would line the tables. The ultimate story I thought distasteful was about the women of the church circle knitting blankets for the refugees in Tanzania. But, when I spoke with my mom that evening, she started telling me she had been at the circle that day knitting blankets for those same refugees.

I just couldn't see the humor in it at the time; all of that was part of my cultural programming. Now, I can look back and laugh with everyone else. I have many things from my upbringing to be thankful for, including my strong cultural roots, and my idyllic summers at the most beautiful pristine Lake Vermilion, my favorite place on earth. I can now see how many aspects of my upbringing were typical of my ethnic heritage that had been ingrained for generations.

However, the warmth and concern my parents focused on the congregation didn't always find its way into our home. I learned resilience. We were, to be honest, stoic, independent, driven, and reserved. Only good emotions were to be expressed, by children, that is. For mothers, apparently, it sometimes was a different story. Difficult things were not discussed. Children were to be seen and not heard. A conflict was to be avoided at all costs, except in the home. No one was better or worse than another, and it was not okay to be showy or to boast. Keeping up appearances mattered the most, at all costs, even to our relationships within the family. The family was supposed to be all about love. We all loved one another; therefore, love was to be assumed; it was not necessary to show it, or say it, or feel it. We were supposed to just know that we were loved.

Following a prescribed cultural social etiquette was especially important because we were the minister's family, and we had to present the right image. My mother made her "suggested corrections" to help me fit what was expected. As a child, I remember receiving corrections far more than words of approval or acknowledgment. I know that my mom based her behavior on the subconscious programming she had received as a child, which was based on the culture and environment she was raised in. That culture demanded a lot, especially from the children. In the world I grew up in, emotional needs were not seen as equal to the behavioral demands, nor even significant in comparison. As an adult, I can see this very clearly. As a child, the challenging expectations she had for my behavior and the assumptions about feelings became the subconscious programs from which I formed my negative beliefs about myself. I was a highly sensitive child, some of my experiences were probably magnified as they reverberated throughout my being.

While my upbringing seemed to be the norm at the time, when I look back, I can see how much the messages I was given were rooted in cultural and religious beliefs, affecting my subconscious mind in specific ways. Now, I don't need to see it so personally, but, as a child feeling it and taking it in, I was not afforded that luxury.

It is my sincere prayer that what I am sharing is not out of judgment and is not asking for an ounce of sympathy, but instead, is shared with the hope that it will offer answers for others as they sort through the levels of their subconscious programming. I have found healing. I want others to find it too.

With my sensitive ways and my artistic nature, I interpreted my mother's "corrections" to mean that I was a particular disappointment. I remember feeling like I heard complaints about what I did, and what I needed to do—to *be* more. Not surprisingly, as I grew up, I began to show patterns of self-doubt and insecurity. No matter how successful I became, no matter how many accolades I gained, or what world-class stages I performed on, there was always a little voice in the back of my mind whispering, *that's not right. You weren't good enough.*

It's ideal for a child to grow up in an encouraging culture that helps them become a self-confident and capable adult. A child needs to learn to be steady, organized, and predictable, where what they do is celebrated, and all their needs are supported. They need to feel that there is enough time, money, and energy, for what they want to explore. It is great if they experience parents who model self-care and balance in all areas of their lives. They need extra support in areas where they might struggle, in areas that don't come naturally like perhaps, being organized with their activities, time, and things. A child needs encouragement to grow confident and in charge of their world from an early age.

My reality changed in my early teens when I began to play the viola. Even early on, my viola helped me become the master of my world. I am deeply grateful that I found my passion and dream, which guided me through so much of my life. My dream didn't mean it was filled with 100% success, as the world's eyes would view it. Instead, it helped me have purpose and feel inspired to move through, to move on, and to conquer. It is my prayer for everyone; that you will connect to your own source of hope. When it came to music, nothing would stop me, even the many times set-backs "should" have. Here are some of the rewards, against all odds, of my persistence and faith: I received full scholarships for three summers at the Aspen Music Festival and graduated from high school early to attend the Institute de Hautes Etudes Musicale in Montreux, Switzerland. Later, I earned a bachelor's degree and a master's degree from the Juilliard School in New York and another master's degree from Yale University, followed by a Ph.D. from New York University. I have performed for many years at Carnegie Hall with the New York Pops, and I have performed in Europe and Japan and even in the Middle East.

As you can see, my life has been good. Nevertheless, like everyone, I have experienced plenty of problems, limitations, and undesirable consequences. After years of soul-searching and therapy and feeling out of balance, I can see now how these issues were traceable to some undesirable patterns I learned unintentionally during my early childhood, and that have been held in my subconscious mind. I share this to assure you: the patterns of the past and the limitations imposed by the subconscious mind can be overcome, and you can change your future.

As we move through the SoundPath method and techniques, it is important to remember that the subconscious programs running your life need to be explored. This does not mean making detailed descriptions of incidents, but noting how they made you feel—like themes and a synopsis, rather than re-living the story. Our goal is to use vibrations to re-write and re-wire the negative subconscious patterns we learned by observance and experience through our early years.

Our parents influence our self-identity because we're so dependent on them as children. They represent a higher source of power, just short of "God", in the mind of a small child. When one's parents don't seem to believe in them, or aren't able to fully support a child emotionally because of their predispositions and priorities, a host of negative messages flood a child's being, taking up residence deep in the subconscious mind and creating core beliefs. Those beliefs shape thoughts about themselves, and what they believed others felt about them, including not only their parents, but even God.

Our subconscious beliefs are incredibly powerful, and I believe, are primarily responsible for holding us back from accomplishing some of our deepest desires. The biologist, Bruce Lipton, explains how 95 percent of all decisions we make arise from the programming of our subconscious minds. Dr. Lipton demonstrated this theory using a palm-sized black rectangle with a very tiny white dot in the middle. He explained that the tiny white dot was ten times larger than the amount of information that is processed by the conscious mind, and the black rectangle represented the amount of information processed by the subconscious mind.

To exhibit the frustrating and ineffective process of trying to change our subconscious habits with our conscious mind, Dr. Lipton used an example of a jukebox that's programmed with the core beliefs and habits that we learned in childhood. When someone is at the jukebox, and it's playing the wrong song, that person could get really upset with the jukebox. He could scream at it, swear at it, and kick it. But, these actions wouldn't have any effect on what music is being played.

This is what happens when we use our conscious mind to try to change habits and patterns ingrained in our subconscious. We can be upset with what's happening in our lives, or an annoying habit we hate. We can try everything we can think of to fix the problem, but somehow nothing changes. Why is that? Because, wanting something to change and having the proper tools to change it, a quarter and a song playlist, are two different things.

The subconscious mind is the wellspring of our fundamental convictions about the world and the patterns that shape our interactions. It's from this place that we attract the people and situations destined to influence our lives. If our primary beliefs are forged from a sense of inherent self-worth, confidence, connection, trust, and unconditional love, then we vibrate at a level that attracts more of the same. When the inevitable pitfalls of life arise, the resilience we need to overcome them stems from a deep-seated faith in ourselves and others.

But, if our beliefs center around unworthiness and fear, they will keep us from experiencing lasting happiness or fulfilling our potential, no matter how much effort we put in at the surface level. And, in fact, we attract and experience more and more of what we know at increasing levels of intensity as our ineffective frustration accelerates.

Our core beliefs, whether mainly positive or mainly negative, act like the bass notes in a piece of music. Bass notes are the root, structural, and fundamental note in a chord. As the lowest structural note is played, bass notes are what the higher frequencies ride on or bounce off of. Most people put all their attention on the "melodies" of life (how we present ourselves, the things we want to achieve, etc.). But, it's the lowest notes, the unseen core beliefs, that control those melodies and decide whether we overcome obstacles and harmful patterns to accomplish our goals, or not.

Bass notes are crucial to any musical composition because they give structure to the melody. Often, however, we put too much attention and focus on the melody, without realizing the importance of the bass line. It must be human nature to focus on what is most noticeable or apparent, what seems most distinguishable and memorable. It would take a trained musician to be able to notice and even describe the entire chord progression in this way. But, the piece of music can only be fully heard and enjoyed when the melody is out front, and the chords are moving along with it, supporting the music, holding it up, grounding it.

We must become like highly trained musicians, who can recognize and appreciate the bass notes in a piece of music, strengthening the foundation, so that our melodies can soar. To do so, you must conduct a rigorous personal inquiry. What part do you play in your troubles? Do you hold feelings of helplessness, anger, resentment, or fear? What is it about? Ask for help from your Higher Power for understanding, and to imagine what it would feel like to feel stronger. Answering these kinds of questions is a crucial part of learning to tune your instrument. It's also one of the most important steps in raising your vibration, by calling forth the information that you'll need to understand the origin of some of your beliefs.

The harmonic, also known as overtones, is another musical example of how notes are built upon the bass. The fundamental note heard is one of an ascending series of sonic components that sound, although mostly imperceptible, above a clearly audible fundamental pitch. In other words, a certain "sounding" note includes a number of higher frequencies, making up the harmonic spectrum of the sound, that combine to form the sound we are hearing. The pitch we hear is called the fundamental. If the bass note is out of tune, none of the overtones are activated; they are missing.

These terms and concepts are significant as we learn and practice SoundPath techniques. For instance, on a viola, a note needs to be played in tune with a good tone quality to activate the full range of the harmonic spectrum on top of the sounding fundamental pitch. This allows for resonant sympathetic vibrations which magnify the depth and beauty of the note. Without this, the note is missing the supporting tones, and it sounds dead; there is no resonance ringing.

Some major core beliefs come to light as lessons that we came into this lifetime to learn. These lessons can be as profound as they are painful at times. It can also be disconcerting to believe you've mastered a certain challenge, only to have it pop up again later in life and under a different guise. Generally speaking, we're released from the impact of a negative core belief in stages. We only release the deepest layers when we're ready to do so. It would be too shocking and disruptive to release a fundamental core belief suddenly, without the mental and emotional preparation to handle such an abrupt change. As we're being guided by our Higher Power, we only release what we're ready to let go of and integrate into a new way of being.

This can be an extremely challenging process. Most of us can describe a time that a core belief impeded our progress in reaching a goal. I've certainly had this experience at many points in my life. I have often, in the past, felt inadequate in comparison to other people. I felt that I needed to earn love by doing and by becoming more because I myself wasn't enough. These feelings were driven by a big core belief: "I am not worthy of my Higher Power's unconditional love." As I released this idea, and replaced it with the belief that I *am* worthy of my Higher Power's unconditional love, I received many higher vibrational opportunities and relationships both personal and in business.

Because I believed the lie that "I am defective," I attracted people who looked down on me, devalued me, and took advantage of me, even as I strived to serve them. I felt like I needed other people to protect me and to decide what I was worthy of having. This prevented me from seeing and fully using my unique set of gifts. I now believe I am powerful, and my gifts are to be used to heal and serve others, and I do so in a way that's uplifting and positive for me as well.

I no longer need to be a "slave" to others' needs and desires, putting them before my own. Replacing this core belief has allowed me to experience true self-love and self-respect. I am aware of my worth in a healthy way. My change requires others to relate to me differently, and it feels awesome! I can freely claim my gifts and share them in effective ways.

Releasing and changing a core belief is very liberating, but reminders still do come up in my life. I continue to use all the SoundPath tools to keep myself "tuned up."

All my relationships—with my parents, my siblings, my husband, and my kids—have transformed. It doesn't mean that they, or I, don't "forget" and slip back into old patterns such as "not being seen." And, sometimes, what I do for them is taken for granted. But, it no longer affects me in the same way. I don't respond to the old triggers, so either right then or soon afterward, the behavior shifts. And, when it doesn't shift right away, I am not affected. This gives me the freedom to continue growing without setbacks and to create room in my life for very supportive people who love and understand who I am, even when I forget.

The power of replacing negative core beliefs can even have dramatic physical effects. The woman at the New York Expo who'd suffered a stroke and facial paralysis after having suffered from many years of abuse is one of my favorite examples of this. Once she shared her deepest trauma, that she was raped when she was a child and that she'd never shared this information with anyone, and allowed the vibrations from the music to percolate within her, she experienced instantaneous healing.

The woman's core belief was that she was unworthy of pure love and protection from her Higher Power. This belief was pulled out and replaced, along with the deep feelings of shame and guilt for believing that she was responsible for what had happened to her as an innocent child. After her belief was shifted, her face completely freed up, and she could smile and talk normally. Seeing her smile is something that I will always remember so clearly. Having a new ability—and new reasons—to smile is what it is all about!

We used her willingness to be vulnerable and share the traumatic memories that had been etched into her conscious mind, while connecting with the vibrations of the universe, our Higher Power, to shift the energy on this deep core belief. This type of result is more readily accessible in private sessions. But, I believe, and I ask you to believe, that your Higher Power can direct the vibrations and shift from dissonance to resonance. We have the ability to create change as we tap into the vibrating strings connecting us to our Highest Power.

Another tool is the science of kinesiology, or muscle testing, which demonstrates whether the subconscious mind is switched on or off when the core belief is stated. If you have never tried muscle testing, here is how you do it. Enlist the help of a partner and extend your arm straight out from your side. Ask your partner to state your question or belief and press down on your arm while you resist. When the body or subconscious mind believes the statement, it gives you a "yes." The arm remains strong and can't be pushed down easily. If the answer is "no," your arm will go weak.

To muscle test on your own, make a circle with your thumb and a weak finger and hold it tightly. Insert two fingers from your other hand, say "yes," and try to pry them apart. The circle should hold steady. Now, do the same and say "no." You should be able to separate your thumb from your finger. Notice how your body responds; some respond in the opposite fashion. Now you can ask yes and no questions to see what your body/subconscious mind believes.

Muscle testing is a visible sign, kind of a tangible proof, of whether the core belief has been changed on the subconscious level. It isn't essential to the healing or tuning itself. Sometimes, our minds can try to interfere, which I can tell when I am working with a client because the testing becomes invalid. However, this often can be a very helpful tool to understand some of the negative themes that we are using the sound and vibrations to release and replace. It is fun to test afterward and witness and feel the change.

I was fortunate to have training in Brain Gym®, a system that uses kinesiology and exercises to balance the left and right brain for optimal functioning. These exercises can help you get "into the zone" at any time you want to focus. They call it being "switched on." This is an excellent tool to add as we are focusing on discovering and re-patterning our subconscious programs. Here are a few of the exercises I learned:

- As you march in place, cross the "mid-line" of your body and alternately tap your knee with your opposite hand for twenty times on each side.

- Standing, cross one leg over the other, cross your arms, and clasp your hands, palms facing each other. Now, twist them and place your hands on your chest while you place the tip of your tongue behind your top teeth, hold to the count of twenty while you take deep breaths.

Rub below your collarbone with your thumb and first finger of one hand. It can be very tricky to ascertain whether there is any objective truth to our core beliefs, or whether we believe the things that we do simply because it's what we've been told to believe. Ultimately, we want to take responsibility for our growth points and the things we can improve on while releasing harmful and unhelpful ideas—things we've been told about ourselves that may or may not be true. It's a big step to let go of mistreatment, and, instead, claim your responsibility at this moment. An older adult can still be emotionally handicapped because of a caregiver's statement, so many years later. It becomes part of their identity; they may have developed coping mechanisms that are perhaps unhealthy, but still part of life as they know it.

When I want to change a core belief, I first ask my Higher Power to show me what I really believe. The muscle testing helps me verify the responses I get intuitively. Then, I ask that everything that's happened as a result of this idea is pulled and replaced with a positive belief. Often, saying this prayer results in showing the memory of a particular way of being treated like a child that created the incorrect and interfering belief. I can then ask my Higher Power to teach me all of the lessons I need to learn before finally releasing it. One of the beauties of the SoundPath method is that it only minimally involves the conscious mind, as the vibrations work in the subconscious.

By setting the proper intentions for our highest and best, surrendering to our Higher Power, and releasing what no longer serves us, the vibrations introduced into a healing session will be guided to seek out what needs to shift within our subconscious. The resulting changes allow the dissonance to resolve, shifting things into alignment, while bypassing our conscious thinking mind.

Questioning and intention-setting are, of themselves, powerful tools of self-discovery and healing. But, adding the element of vibrational attunement, is what actually re-routes the worn pathways in the brain. Understanding the effects of sound vibration can help anyone to access the ability to connect to our Higher Power, letting go of the analytical conscious mind. Since vibrations are made up of energy, when we tap into the Creator-Source-Universal energy, the energy that we access comes from that higher level of attunement. It can shift the low vibrations that aren't helping us and replace them with higher frequencies that evoke positive change.

The brain has different states and related functions which correspond to vibrational levels of frequency. There is new research about the Gamma brainwave state (above 40Hz) linked to sudden insights and quick processing of information, similar to what Dr. Lipton calls "energy super-learning." The other known states of vibrations include the following typical ranges:

Beta brainwave state (14-40Hz)—normal consciousness while awake and alert. This can help with focused reasoning and function. It can also be heard as that nagging loop of thoughts that contribute to stress and anxiety.

Alpha brainwave state (7.5-14Hz)—deep relaxation wave, when eyes are closed, and you are meditating or daydreaming. It is the beginning of accessing your subconscious mind. This is an effective state for the work with SoundPath because your memory, imagination, ability to visualize, access intuition (especially at the lower level) and learning is heightened.

Theta brainwave state (4-7.5Hz)—light meditation and sleeping. This is the state when you are drifting off to sleep and as you are waking up. This is a powerful state for our healing re-patterning because it gives you brief access to your subconscious mind and is a powerful opportunity for brain re-patterning. This also includes the REM (rapid eye movement) dream state. This is the level that holds your subconscious programs and patterns, as well as where you can have deep insights, creativity, and inspiration.

Delta brainwave state (0.5-4Hz)—the deep, dreamless sleep with access to your unconscious mind, the universal truths, and collective consciousness. Your body uses this state to rejuvenate and to access deep healing.

I keep a notebook and pen by my bed so I can write down my realizations from my theta state as I wake up. I have learned that once my conscious mind is fully awake, rather than being more alert and able to process these thoughts, they elude me and disappear.

In addition to self-inquiry and intention setting, certain meditations are helpful in developing a deeper understanding of our core beliefs and where they come from, as well as the ability to allow the vibrations to make any changes needed. I am very blessed to have done extensive training with Vianna Stibal, the creator of Theta Healing®, an amazingly effective modality. The following exercise is inspired by a process that Vianna refers to as, "going up to the Seventh Plane." This exercise helps us reach a meditative state where we have more connection with our Higher Power, a place where "super-learning" and awareness is invited.

It is best to do this as you start any of the meditative exercises that help to observe, acknowledge, and release negative subconscious patterning and replace it with positive beliefs and unconditional love.

1. Sit comfortably; feet on the floor; notice how you feel, your vibrational level; place hands comfortably on your lap, preferably palms up with thumb lightly touching your first finger; breathe deeply in through the nose; pause; exhale through the mouth; repeat a few times.

2. Feel your energy centered just above your stomach, feel it rise up through and above your head, continue to see it rise higher and higher, above the room and building that you're in, through the sky, beyond the planets, feel it rise until you see white and feel peace and energy from the highest place.

3. Asking a key question (i.e., where does my belief in unworthiness come from? Why do I keep inviting the same types of people into my life?), then pause and listen. Feel the physical sensation that's created by the negative

pattern you wish to replace and wonder about a time in your childhood when you felt this way. What were you being told? What happened that caused you to create and need to re-create this belief to feel okay? What were you taught about your worth and your experience and definition of love?

4. Now, ask your Higher Power to remove that belief. See the negative belief rise out of you and continue to rise until it is dispersed through the white light and it disappears.

5. Ask your Higher Power to teach you all of your lessons and replace that space with unconditional love.

6. See the place that it was removed from fill up with beautiful, white unconditional love. Feel and imagine your new pathway filled with freedom and ease.

7. Notice how you feel, your vibrational level, and give thanks.

Observe the thoughts and feelings that arise with this healing experience. Be prepared to write down any insights you receive. Then, ask yourself: "What healthy ways can I reach the feelings of love and acceptance to reinforce my new neural pathways?"

The long-standing negative subconscious patterns are like a horrible, ugly, dissonant noise, similar to a horn honking or traffic; as it is replaced with love, you can listen to beautiful, peaceful music filled with rich, supportive harmonies.

This is an important step in releasing damaging core beliefs while retaining the core beliefs that serve us well. This will be repeated whenever you observe interfering negative patterns.

In this process, the vibrations will know what to do. But, there are also specific physical exercises to help access the answers desired from our self-inquiry. It's always best to start any of these exercises by breathing in through our nose, feeling the stomach expand, holding the breath, and then releasing the breath through the mouth. Feel yourself fill up with love and then release anything that causes dissonance within. Such simple meditations push our internal pause button, allowing us to take the time to connect with our Higher Power. These inner "conversations" will restore the soul, so we must be especially mindful of leaving time to listen and receive guidance, as well as peace.

When we make our choices from this meditative brainwave state, we start moving on a new "wavelength," one that allows supportive decisions and great opportunities to enter our "flow." This ties into the explanation of neuroplasticity and the brain's ability to create new pathways to replace the pathways of pain.

Our brains have specific neural signatures for the pain we experience. Over time, the thoughts and feelings we habitually entertain wear deep grooves into our neural pathways. Our synapses, which are communication areas between neurons, have incredibly plastic properties that are essential to memory and learning. This is exciting! When we think new thoughts and feel new feelings, we can get our synapses firing along different neural pathways. So, even though the memory traces of painful emotions and experiences aren't easily changed or erased, it can be done. A chosen detour can be created, and with practice, the mind will choose this pathway as the pathway of pain lies dormant. Even in the woods, a pathway needs to be continually used, or the weeds and bushes grow up and erase the once-used pathway.

In the book, *Unlearn Your Pain*, Howard Schubiner tells the true story of a physician whose leg was severely injured when his Army helicopter was shot down. After many surgeries, his leg was almost healed, except for occasional flare-ups of pain. The doctor's wife finally made the connection that the pain in her husband's leg was triggered when a helicopter flew by. Her husband wasn't even aware of it, but his subconscious mind was triggering the trauma that then recreated the resulting symptoms.

Fortunately, we can "distract" the brain's memory and its reliance on specific pathways associated with pain, creating new, pleasant, and positive pathways instead. After attention and use is taken from the negative pathway, it atrophies, and the mind will focus on using the new pathway that's working much better.

This is why vibrational attunement is so effective; it creates new grooves that are then reinforced through the emotional and spiritual work mentioned previously.

When we have awareness and the willingness to grow, we can learn how to change the patterns that have created the most persistent blocks. For me, the blocks would show up as a discouraging voice in my head. *"Don't do that"*, the voice would say. *"It'll never work!"* But, over time, when the voice would come into my head, I became aware that I could talk to it. I could challenge what the voice was saying and question the stories that I'd created in my mind based on it. Was the voice based on truth? Or, was it based on fear caused by what someone else said or did to me?

We must always remember that we're separate from our thoughts and separate from our past. What we think about creates more of it, so we need to use the brain's incredible powers of manifestation to bring about change; we must be disciplined in redirecting harmful thoughts toward a path that is more honest and truthful. After some time, the new pattern creates new habits that will form our new positive core beliefs. From this place, the subconscious mind will be able to make healthier choices. Over time, the ability to make better, healthier choices will happen automatically with ease.

Visioning can help accelerate this process. Try thinking of a creepy memory like, for instance, lifting up an old rug with huge, ugly bugs crawling out and slimy things growing on it. Then, replace it with your most beautiful memory or thought. For example, I deeply love flowers. So, I envision the upsetting, tormenting thought as a flower that I pluck from the ground by the root and hand over to God.

This belief work gives the gift of an instant release and healing when we believe. To integrate the change within you, and all of the areas and habits affected, use tools like sound/vibration therapy and visioning along with time, focus, and patience for the results to be solidified into new subconscious patterns. You, with help from your Higher Power, are creating new neural pathways, and it is well worth it! I've seen countless miracles and have witnessed so much beauty.

In my own life, I'm finally coming to deeper awareness and healing, which has brought incredible joy and many positive things into my life. But, I've also come to understand that other layers of the lessons stemming from these beliefs and patterns may show up. When you think you've learned all that a particular lesson has to teach, it will pop up in some other area in your life, in a way that is unexpected, to receive deeper healing. It's best to keep tuning up and be prepared for any necessary adjustments and further patterns that need to be released.

Because of my subconscious programming, I dealt with a longstanding belief that I can't and won't do anything of value. In the past, this belief has caused me to act as my own worst enemy. I've done a tremendous amount of healing work around this false idea, finally gaining my freedom. Yet, it came up again for me recently in a very unexpected way. Someone close to me had a major health crisis; they were close to death and needed help. But, somehow it brought out some of the worst devaluing patterns I had experienced as a child. Anything I did to help wasn't noticed, or, if it was noticed, it wasn't enough. I was never OK. At first, it felt terrible. How could it be that after all my growth, all the tools I'd learned and used, and how much I'd changed over the years that I could still find myself in the same circumstance? How could I be still suffering so much?

It felt so disheartening. But, after a while, I noticed that the old scripts weren't having the same effect on me. In fact, I was able to step back and witness the negative interactions without being drawn in by them in the same way. With a new level of awareness, the deeper lesson became clear. I realized how many people I'd allowed into my life who had the very same dynamics. My deep healing awareness came to me like a gift, with an awareness of the grace I had been given. I can feel the love beneath all of the circumstances and can hold onto all that matters, which is love. This is an example of tuning, finding harmony and alignment, which replaces the disharmony and imbalance.

It was then that I saw clearly that this pattern was part of an illusion. I called people into my life to play a familiar pattern of not being enough. However, this twisted paradigm of seeking approval to fill the dark hole of "not being enough" reinforced the opposite results. Striving to feel complete and whole by outside validation wasn't possible. Because, for one thing, the validation that we seek can only come from within.

As I started moving away from these difficult relationships and people, I was able to make progress in areas of my life that had been stalled for years. I could claim my dreams, instead of enlisting people to create interfering sabotage. The lessons, though painful, had enabled me to move on. I had to let go of so many people, at least in the way that I'd previously interacted with them. The group of people "still standing" with love and support was not very large. But, the relationships that I maintain today are infinitely healthier. And, I know that if I ever invite any of the negative influences close to me again, and they begin to push me down that rabbit hole of negativity, I'll be able to catch it and stop it quickly. Now, my loss can be found and the hole can be filled.

Before I was seven, I created a core belief so profound that it impacted me even into middle age. It became part of my basic "computer programming," a central part of my underlying system that was playing, still. But, because I was able to initiate a process guided by God that allowed vibrations to go to where the healings and shifts were needed, I was able to shift my response to a childhood trigger. I was able to fill the dark hole with love.

This is SoundPath: bypassing the conscious mind and changing the root causes of our conflicts at the level where it matters the most.

FOUR
TUNING UP

The practice of being in tune begins with pausing to cultivate deep listening and mindfulness. As we become aware of being aware, we become able to focus our attention on the harmonics and the overtones woven into every aspect of life. When we step back and observe ourselves, we can begin to recognize the areas of dissonance and see how to shift those areas.

Listen to the spaces between each breath. What do you hear? Does the volume of your thoughts feel like it fills up every part of your head? Is the loudest sound the most important one? Do you listen first before you add to the noise around you? Are you guided by impulse or intuition? How does this apply to your thoughts and actions throughout your day? What is the difference between sound and silence? Could we hear a sound without the silence? Is there silence within a sound?

Sound is born from silence. In every aspect of life, silence precipitates connection and the quality of our communication. For example, the quality of our leadership is directly related to the level that we can embrace the silence within. A great leader must be able to tune in and listen to the messages and directions of those we lead, starting with ourselves.

Tuning in means slowing down and finding moments to sit in silence, connect with your breath, and feel its rhythm. Practice doing this as a mediation each day. Listen to what your heart is trying to communicate, the meaning that takes shape in the space between the words. Sound can sometimes drown out meaning, while allowing space can reveal what's truly important, especially in uncertainty. The quiet voice brings us the clearest message.

But, it's nearly impossible to hear and accurately understand the messages we need to receive when our hearts, minds, and spirits are out of tune. Think of it this way: when you drive your car for long periods of time without going in for a tune-up, the mechanics start to break down. The longer you wait, the more problems pop up in the various systems. Most of us have been in that position at one time or another. First, you need an oil change and some other fluids added so the car will run properly. Or, maybe a window won't close, so some draft blows into the car, and you can't secure it.

The problems are annoying, but the car still runs, so you're in no hurry to spend time and money on a mechanic. But, then the brakes start squeaking, and the alignment veers off. Later, the engine skips and the muffler breaks. After a while, the issues that used to be minor annoyances have now become real safety hazards. Eventually, the car, which could have been easily fixed in the beginning, becomes inoperable. Each thing that's "out of tune" impacts your ability to drive and to be safe or to function. It wouldn't matter how desperately you might want to get some-where. Now, you can't travel freely without risking a breakdown in the middle of the road.

When a person is out of tune, the disconnect can take many different forms. Sometimes, it looks like being out of shape and not eating in a healthy, well-balanced way. Disharmony can show up as stress, exhaustion, agitation, or irritability. Some people feel consumed with resentment and anger over past wrongs. Others contend with financial strains or disagreements and misunderstandings with loved ones. Still, others walk through life filled with fear and mistrust, being treated badly and taken for granted by people they care about. Repeatedly experiencing people misusing your kindness and goodwill is a sure sign that you are out of alignment in some area.

For example, I had a repeating pattern based on a core belief that other people knew more than me and were better than me—they were more talented, more intelligent, more capable. I believed I needed to serve others to earn the opportunity to work with them. For me, and probably for many others, my deepest core belief was that God felt this way about me, too. And, when I needed help from someone in my life, it was extremely difficult to get up the courage to ask, since deep down I didn't believe I deserved it. This attitude got me into difficult situations where other people began to reflect back to me, my own inner beliefs. Others stopped hearing me and I was completely out of tune.

Eventually, I came to my senses and realized that I was capable of doing so much more than I ever gave myself credit for. My peers in the music industry were just that—peers. They weren't superiors looking down on me. In fact, I received much more admiration and respect from others than I did in my estimation of myself.

When I started to reclaim the power I'd so carelessly given away, it didn't go over big with the few people who'd gotten used to dealing with me in my self-doubting, disempowered state. I had to dig deeper than I ever had to find the formative core beliefs that still needed to be cleared and replaced. Like peeling back the layers of an onion, it took years of work to allow me to access more profound levels of understanding. But, with time and patience, my practice finally began to bring about significant change.

Now, I know that I must remain in my truth, no matter what. I do believe that I can go into new relationships with my eyes open widely, and I'll be able to set boundaries and parameters with more clarity and confidence. I need to be true to myself first and trust that God has a plan and that the right people will come to me. I am making room for this to be true. Today, I can be very grateful for my parents and siblings and the various people in my life who taught me the invaluable lesson that I am more than okay. I am much more than enough.

To achieve this kind of awareness, we must first step out of the status quo. This means leaving behind the kind of "lowest common denominator" behaviors that keep us out of tune. Bickering, gossiping, comparing, compromising oneself to appease others, feeling excessive strain, and experiencing an imposed need to please others, are all behaviors that will lead you to disharmony. Instead, step out of the defined box. Stand in the awareness of how you honestly feel—physically, mentally, spiritually, and emotionally. Can you imagine something that you would like changed? Would you like to feel differently? It is safe to look truthfully at your life because you're in charge—and you have the power to change the things that no longer serve you.

Cultivating awareness is key to finding harmony and being in tune because it represents the first step in making a change. Otherwise, we eventually just get numb to our discomfort. We might notice that we feel sad, stressed, out of energy, uninspired, or tired, all the time. But, then what? It may even seem easier not to ask the questions or notice what's off because of the fear that bringing light and awareness to your issues will only make them worse.

A desire to feel better is the catalyst for creating lasting change. You must be able to hear the noise that sounds bad—dissonant and out of tune—before you can adjust it to feel the harmony of things finally falling into place. So many people accept the "status quo" as the only choice or the default, without stopping to wonder what else might be out there.

Consider the analogy of tuning a viola. The process of tuning such a wonderful and delicate musical instrument mirrors what goes on inside us mentally, emotionally, and spiritually. Each time before I play, even throughout the day, I need to check the tuning of my viola. It gets out of tune because the various woods react to the humidity in the air differently. The strings are wound onto a peg that turns inside of a peg box, which holds the string in place once it's in tune. The pegs are shaped like cones, and you need to push in while you turn the peg, so it will stay secure once the correct pitch has been found. Otherwise, the peg will slip down once you've turned it and let go.

Changes in temperature and humidity cause the wood to swell or shrink. Moreover, the changes in the wood happen in different ways because the viola is created from different woods. The pegs are made from ebony. The top of the viola is spruce, and the back and the peg box are carved from maple. The pegs get looser in lower humidity and tighter in higher humidity. In other words, the body changes in direct relation to the changes in its environment.

When I pick up my instrument, I use a tuning fork, or a digital tuner, to find an "A"—440 MHz. Then, I play the open strings together, A and D, and adjust the D string until it locks into the open sound of a perfect fifth. I adjust the peg by turning back and forth, wedging it in between two fingers of my left hand while the other fingers stay on the other side so that I can push in towards the peg box while I'm tuning. I must make certain that the adjustments of the peg stay in place when I let go. You can hear when it arrives; the harmony of the sound waves locking together are felt on every level. When using a tuner, sometimes the red light turns to green when the pitch is correct. But, tuning the open strings by ear is more accurate.

Our lives have many different parts that change, according to changes in our environment. Start to collect your special set of SoundPath techniques that can help you tune-up throughout the day. Make this your practice, preparing you for any "performance" that life brings to you. Enjoy "playing" your unique sounds on your well-tuned beautiful instrument, you.

However, on occasion, even a top performer will play out of tune. She may be just a little off. If she isn't fully present, if she isn't fully in the moment, if her thinking mind concentrates too much on technique or becomes distracted, she may slide out of tune. And, she may not be aware of it. But, many people in the audience will feel it's a little off, or they may not like it without knowing why, while others—with a trained ear or not, listening attentively or not—will know it's "out of tune."

It is no different with us. If we don't have the keen ear or patience to focus on finding the right pitch, life can become a touch out of tune. We may not notice. But, others will.

The image of the green light appearing when the correct intonation, or note, arrives is a good image to remember when tuning into ourselves and life. Do you see the red or green light on the tuner? Is this the note that you want to keep and use in the melodies that you will continue to correct and live?

As we go through life, different parts of us are changing and need to readjust. Some may be stuck in a place of interfering disharmony. The discord may be faint, maybe almost inaudible, but the vibrations don't interact to allow harmony and ease. When we're out of tune, we aren't able to express ourselves fully because we lack the ease of functioning. Our sense of wellbeing may become warped by environmental factors beyond our control.

Sometimes, an instrument can get very out of tune if it hasn't been played in a while or it's had a drastic temperature change (a viola can never be left in a car, for instance). Sometimes, drastic misalignments can come about due to the ordinary ups, downs, and changes that happen in life. For instance, my instrument is very sensitive to heat and humidity. I recently played an outdoor concert in extreme heat and humidity, and I had to pay one thousand dollars to have my viola repaired and adjusted afterward. One time, I played a concert without air conditioning during the summer in an old church. The temperature was well over one hundred degrees with high humidity. Just a short amount of time spent in those conditions caused seams to burst open on the instrument and cost me almost three hundred dollars to get it fixed.

When extreme or traumatic events occur in life, most people realize they need to regroup and reconnect to heal and restore their equilibrium. But, in contrast, most people never think about the myriad ways our everyday conditions and circumstances are creating fundamental changes in us. Taking the time for regular tune-ups and self-care is critical to our wellbeing, no matter how the misalignment occurs.

Tuning has two steps: first, the instrument needs to be adjusted and put into alignment. Then, it needs frequent daily tuning of the strings to activate the overtones—that blending of all the sounds required to make a particular note. This represents the daily challenges we face and the activities that help us navigate those challenges successfully. Sustaining a daily practice as a means of living consciously makes an incredible impact in our ongoing quest to fill the holes in our hearts and play the missing notes.

For me, playing the missing notes means that I am pausing, listening deeply, hearing, and acknowledging the pain of absence in my heart. The next step is crucial to demonstrating change: I no longer ask someone else to fill in those notes, someone that I think is more talented or better equipped. I no longer ask someone else to explain to me what they hear is missing. Instead, I listen, and I ask my Higher Power to help me fill in the empty spaces so that I am whole and have a full range of notes to sing my songs. It's a wonderful reminder that our answers lie within; no one else can sing our song, and certainly, they can't sing it better than we can.

When the note is out of tune, that means it's missing some of the harmonics. When the harmonics haven't been activated, the sound is weak and flat; sometimes it is called "dead," with less resonance and less depth. The result is unpleasant because the notes cannot make subtle changes to "color" and shape the phrase. An out-of-tune note isn't that note at all; it becomes a wrong note. Someone who is tone-deaf wouldn't be as affected, but this is like telling a lie; the wrong thoughts and words have been expressed. Likewise, if you have a limited ability to communicate—a smaller vocabulary, a speech impediment, or an unintelligible accent—mutual understanding will be diminished.

Each step in the process relates to our ability to get back in tune after experiencing the trials, obstacles, and heartbreaks of life. When we find ourselves moving through another cycle of our pain and lessons, we can acknowledge the process with gratitude. After all, it takes a growing level of awareness to recognize both the need and the ability to learn from the hard lessons, choosing to step aside from patterns of self-lashings and self-abuse. Instead, we can look up and see that there's a lifeline to grab that will help us to be free from the pain. The lifeline comes from God, who is always there for us with the answers.

But, to hear those answers, we must first release whatever blame, shame, or resentment we may have, for others as well as ourselves. The release allows us to disconnect from any vestiges of the old idea that God was somehow in on our suffering, or the fear that God may hold the same negative ideas about us as our "enemies." Detouring from that pathway of pain helps hone the awareness we are all capable of learning through insight and revelation, rather than sorrow.

This takes effort. In the beginning, it will feel like you're in a canoe, alone, paddling upstream as some strong current tries to pull you back downstream. Giving up would be so natural and easy because the pains of your past are familiar and, therefore, almost comforting. You'll need to constantly remind yourself to choose a new pathway, which you can only travel on when you surrender and receive help from your Higher Power. It's impossible to travel upstream using only your own efforts.

Instead of struggling against the tide of unhelpful habits, step back, take a breath, and honestly ask yourself how you feel. As Dr. Phil would say, "How is this working for you?" Think about the lessons that have been coming back around for your attention. Are they painful or upsetting for you to deal with? Ask yourself if you've ever felt this way before. How many times before? Take another breath and ask yourself to pinpoint the earliest memory when you felt this way. Who was involved in helping to reinforce this feeling? Were you told hurtful things about yourself at a young age? Did you take this on and then add your feelings and story onto it? Did those early lessons and core beliefs make you feel disconnected, unloved, or somehow just "off?"

When we're young, we are forming a definition of who we are in the world. This picture is etched in our being, for better or worse. We need to allow the vibrations to go into those continuous memories and change them. But, we first need to believe, at our very essence, that we are worthy of being healed. The subconscious mind interprets a memory of a past event as if it is happening now. It's in real time, here and now, even if the precipitating event happened decades ago.

The awesome thing, explained by quantum physics, is that in this world of healing the past, present, and future are with us in each moment. The passing of time, in a way, doesn't exist outside our limited, linear sense of time. We can call the experiences and feelings of the past into this moment and surrender them to the healing hand of God. Through our request for healing and the belief in its fulfillment, the energy of creation is activated. It goes in and fills the broken places with unconditional love, and we are changed.

However, this healing must be accepted with belief, not doubt; if you need to question the change and demand "proof," part of the healing may be reversed. This will create another opportunity in the future—when the pattern returns in a new way, and it will—for you to look at the deeper levels of pain that continue block the path to freedom. This doesn't mean that your healing wasn't successful or "real" the first time. But, as we know, we heal in layers. Each time you go to a deeper, more honest level of breaking and releasing unhelpful habits, you will soar a little higher with more freedom, strength, realization, and support. It's a journey—not a destination. So, enjoy the journey as you continually use the tools at your disposal to find new ways to break free.

Meditation is one of the most important tools. It's a practice that can be done throughout the day, anytime you feel like you need to check in and tune up. When I tune in to meditate, I can feel God and my angels and all the support of the saints helping me. When I bow in service, I'm asking God to guide me to the next part of my path. Cultivating this practice over time begins to create an underlying state of meditation, which undergirds all your interactions as you move throughout your day.

Sometimes, this support and guidance enters into my conscious mind as concrete requests. Sometimes I will "hear" pleas for help from others that I'm able to answer. The more confirmations of serendipitous encounters come to me, the more I can see God smiling as these gifts are laid out before me. Meditation is being in a state of receptivity. These gifts of the spirit can only come to you if you're willing and able to receive them with gratitude and grace.

Have you ever had someone expect a gift from you? Isn't it most frustrating when you were already going to give it to them freely? Now, some of the joy has been removed due to the entitled, demanding energy behind the request. When this happens, where does it leave us? Rather than reacting by giving in or rebelling against the demand, being in tune with the Presence invites us to meditate and listen. Ask God if giving your gift is really for the highest and best good of everyone involved. If you do decide to give, you can do so freely, releasing the interference of the ego. God is above our egos, and our souls are beneath it, holding us firmly in grace. Yet, this vital assistance needs to be requested; Spirit doesn't like to interfere but is always ready to help when we ask.

Sit comfortably with your feet on the ground, close your eyes, breathe deeply, and think of yourself in a boat taking you on the journey we call, "life." What type of boat are you in? What type of preparations do you have? Is there enough gas or paddles or are you in a sailboat trusting God to supply the wind? Is it a simple kayak, a speedboat, or a luxury boat? Is it well-kept, or is there a small leak, or even a bigger threatening hole? Have you prepared well? Have you mapped out your course, researched the weather forecast, and eliminated any dangers? Is your equipment sufficient, or have you sabotaged your safety and arrival? Are you to blame; can you be responsible? Do you feel panic, or are you calm as you enjoy the beauty, feel the sunshine on your face, and rest, because you know you've prepared well and you are safely in good hands—in God's hands.

We must reach out and take hold of every opportunity to grow, to adapt and evolve, to seize our dreams. Tuning in to the activation of our dream means thinking about the steps involved in living that dream, turning it from a desire into reality. We know we're in tune with our purpose when we can identify it in great detail, then move toward that dream with practical, small, even tiny, steps. Feel the presence and the fulfillment of that desire. Enjoy the steps that you're led to take; see where they are headed without the need to control every movement. Keep writing down the next steps each time you reach another part of your dream.

Ask God to help you with the direction for your steps. Then, watch the even bigger dream that God unfolds for you! One word of caution: if you feel like you're paddling upstream, with each stroke, ask God to help you realign your dream so that you can feel His assistance along the way. This doesn't mean that you won't have to work. At times, there will be frustration and struggle. But, even then, when you step back, you'll see how you learned another valuable lesson you needed to progress to the next level. Now, you can move forward in the flow, surrounded by support.

Tuning up begins by listening carefully, to hear the messages. As we learn how to tune up and how to maintain good intonation, when the note is in tune, when we are playing music with someone else, we will be able to be in tune individually, and together. As we listen to the other person or the ensemble of several people, we become aware of tuning up to the underlying "bass notes" for everyone. People's melodies on top of their bass notes sometimes don't reveal exactly who they are, because maybe they aren't able to tune in to them.

I had a SoundPath sound healing session with a client last year named, Isabelle, who was suffering from a life-threatening condition that undermined her will to live. Thankfully, she was still willing to participate in this new experience. She found the music to be soothing, but preferred to receive and observe rather than actively participate. Her sister, Patricia, who came to the session, had an extremely resistant, competitive, negative, and critical attitude. As I observed Patricia's behavior, I realized that she felt a need to make other people wrong, and beneath her, so she could feel right; this was her protection. This also allowed her to feel in control as she aimed to be intimidating in her arrogant way. Patricia's behavior reminded me of a porcupine throwing out needles to keep any fearful predators away. This sabotaging negative behavior had an impact on Isabelle's experience and her life. The sisters were competitive even though there was an opposite manifestation of it. One partially masked it with protection and pushed people away while the other was a perfectionist with an extreme misunderstood need to please others. Underneath, both Isabelle's and Patricia's behaviors were polarized beliefs of insecurity, low self-esteem, and fear. These patterns made it difficult to participate and receive what I had to offer.

The sisters were examples of Ying and Yang, as they had such different attitudes. However, my job was to hold a space of unconditional love with the intention of inviting in the highest and best. Patricia was there to teach us to listen to the bass notes beneath someone's behavior. So, I tried to help Isabelle stay connected to truth and have boundaries to keep out negativity. I received a beautiful bonus gift from my Higher Power; as I was walking down the hall after the session, wishing that I could have done even more for the sisters, but trusting that it was all that was needed, a girl and her mom thanked me for the beautiful music they heard, from the next room. "It healed our hearts," they told me. We never know what seeds are planted or how they are going to grow.

The next part of the tune-up process is to begin to work with your overtones. The other night, I watched a television performance by a singer who is deaf. She lost her hearing when she was eighteen. It was so sad to hear the story of how each sound disappeared from her world. But, her parents encouraged her to hang onto her gift of music and singing. Music had been her way of communicating. Singing was her dream. Her light and spirit soared through her heart as she sang from within.

This miraculous young woman used her feet to feel the overtones that vibrated when the note was in tune. Her intonation, the tuning of the pitches, was impeccable. The notes shimmered uniquely, as the overtones locked in her simple, pure sounds. The audience of thousands was enthralled. With many people in tears by the end of her song, they leaped to their feet and cheered as she looked out through her own tears. One judge called her an angel. She simply spontaneously replied in a sincere voice, "I will pray for you."

Because the young woman felt the music, the entire audience could feel it with her. This amazing connection was happening through the overtones and her heart. I believe that overtones ring along in support and amplification of good. When overtones are vibrating in harmony, it feels like you are walking amongst and being supported by the Angels. All the wonderful things that come into our lives—miracles, grace, love, light—are given to us with the choir of Angels by our side, walking with us in service of all that is good. When we're in tune and feel these overtones, they vibrate out from within us. Everyone, even those not physically around us, will feel them on a subconscious level. Remember, frequency operates on the principles of quantum physics or string theory. Physical proximity is irrelevant.

There are many exercises commonly used in sound therapy that can help to get us in tune physically. One, that is particularly powerful, requires that you find an instrument that resonates with you. You can use a drum or other percussion instrument, for instance, a bell, shaker, or rattle. This might mean finding a cast-iron Bundt pan and taking it to a local music store to find a mallet that creates a sound that resonates with you. Or, you can purchase a drum and mallet. If you don't want to spend any money, you can do something as simple as creating a simple shaker by experimenting with the sounds of rice, beans, seeds, etc., and placing them inside a small container. Another idea is to create a drum out of a cylindrical oats container, a bucket, or a box. For more ideas, you can Google, "homemade instruments using recycled materials." Once you have your instrument, you can begin your sound meditation.

Play your instrument in a way that feels relaxing and comfortable to you. Tempo doesn't matter; nor does it matter whether you're playing an identifiable "song." Feel the rhythm reaching deep within you and give yourself over to its patterns. Be aware of the thoughts that arise as you release your subconscious mind over to the music. Pause, then allow yourself to connect to the vibrations and invite them to fill up the spaces that were released in the alignment process. Consciously welcome the feeling of wholeness and wellbeing as you slowly begin winding down.

Toning is another exercise that builds on the previous exercise. Take a deep breath in and release a deep guttural sound, as deep as possible. Feel the vibrations in the part of your body that feels stuck. I often can feel tightness in my throat, which represents my fear to speak up and be heard. Let the vibrations reach every cell in your body and mind, especially places that are stuck and blocked, and let them tune you. With each breath, you'll gradually feel and hear the pitch rise. Continue until you feel you're finished for now. Remember to ask your Higher Power for help in releasing that which is ready to be released and shifted. Healing is done in layers, and it would be much too shocking and uncomfortable to change everything at once. Be grateful for each experience of release and change. Feel the new level of freedom and consciously seek to integrate with it. When you're ready, you can continue.

An exercise that helps in the tuning up process is to create a symphony with several "movements." It can start with a group of people playing as loudly and densely as they can. Slowly, the players transition into sections. Each person will imagine different sections created with a theme based on something like a color or the seasons or whatever inspiration comes through. This is about letting our creativity interact with our intuition and the ability to listen to oneself and others.

Another meditative practice to try is centered on "being here now." This is a practice about being present in the spaces between knowing; "before" and "after" stop being our focal point, as they can only exist and be born if we embrace the current space first. Space is our gift. There's no fear when you rest in between, finding connection, truth, clarity, all-knowingness, and love at the center of it all, in the spaces between.

Inhale deeply and pause before exhaling. Waiting and listening is an active and invaluable state of rest. The power lies in the spaces between. First, become comfortable, breathe deeply, feel your attention rise above your body higher and higher until you can imagine a beautiful bright light. Tune in to how you are feeling. What kind of music would accompany your feeling right now? Is this something you want to hear more or less of? You are the producer, composer, and sound editor. You choose which sections to repeat, which to delete, and what the volume and arrangement will be. Decide how you want to feel; if you want to change, just as in life, create it and take yourself there. Hear the music change in this new mood. Focus on the effects and new creations rather than only repeating well-formed musical scores from the past.

FIVE

HEARING THE MESSAGES OF THE MUSIC

We will never be successful in tuning up our lives if we're not willing to listen to the messages we're receiving about what needs adjustment. Every trial, setback, disappointment, or failure, has within it the potential for growth. Every experience of a broken heart can teach us more about compassion, resilience, and acceptance. Every tragedy creates a space that may be filled with insight and healing, rather than being defined solely by pain and fear. All the things that happen to us represent the music, or the soundtrack, of our lives. The messages in that music offer us revelations, which we can use to change our circumstances for the better. The messages are the grace notes that help us become stronger and wiser in the face of life's challenges.

However, too often we refuse to listen to the subconscious messages we receive because we are often the only person who doesn't see what is happening. This makes it even more upsetting to face them. Negative subconscious coping mechanisms and programming come into play. If we blame, shame, deflect, lie, cheat, or become defensive to avoid self-reflection, it's certain we'll never understand the lessons that are seeking to come through. Healing requires that these coping mechanisms be replaced with the willingness not only to identify those lessons but to act on the Divine counsel we're receiving. Our lifelong health and wellbeing depend on it.

To experience a change in our lives, we need to step back and listen to the music we hear all around. It's like an intuitive soundtrack playing theme music to accompany whatever's happening in your life as you live it, moment by moment. When you tune into your heart and listen closely, what kind of soundtrack do you hear? Is it scary, dissonant music leading to an unknown place with a big, stressful build up? Does the music resolve into peaceful dissonance with beautiful, flowing melodies? Or, do you mainly hear staccato, short, erratic, repetitive, unresolved phrases? What type of music predominates your soundtrack? Upbeat and hopeful or sad and melancholy? Is it your favorite style or someone's else's favorite style that you've been forced to listen to?

Once you begin to hear the specific elements of your music, go deeper and imagine what it represents in your life. For example, if your soundtrack feels loud and violent, can you identify any relationships or situations you face that have the same energy? If the music feels slow or repetitive, ask yourself if you could be in a rut. If so, are there any specific changes you'd like to see and hear? What is beneath the melody supporting it? Then, imagine what else you might want to hear. What does the potential change represent to you? What steps would you need to take toward this change?

Then, ask the most fundamental question: what does transformation sound like?

Imagine that you're sitting in a comfortable chair. Take a few deep breaths in through your nose and out through your mouth. Now, recall two real scenarios from your life, one happy and one sad. Think of them, one at a time, and decide what music you would score for each scene. Start with the happy memory. Recall some music that you know or allow a basic style to come into your mind. Feel the music as you re-experience this scene.

Now, bring up the unhappy scene in your mind's eye. What music do you hear accompanying this scene? Has this scene played in similar ways at different times throughout your life?

Ask yourself: what would need to happen to transform this scene into one with a more positive ending? How would the music need to change? Feel the process and hear the music as it transforms your thoughts, your mood, and eventually, your understanding of the scene that's playing in your mind. Be mindful of what that transformation sounds like. You have the power and the choice. Once you develop the courage, interest, and ability to listen, you'll be able to create a new playlist for your soundtrack.

Listening and being receptive is critical to the tune-up process because if you continue living on auto-pilot, based on what's been pre-programmed in the hard drive of your life, nothing will change. If you keep doing what you've always done, you'll keep being how you've always been and getting the results that you've always received. Without developing the skill of deep listening, it's almost assured that you'll react in the way you always have. It's like listening to the same theme song on repeat when you have the opportunity to upgrade to a premium channel with more choices.

I believe we are co-creators in our lives, and ultimately, the messages we receive are coming directly from our Higher Power. The messages can speak to us through our Angels and guides or our circumstances, laying a host of choices out before us as we walk through life. Depending on how clearly we're able to see and hear what's going on, we can develop the ability to choose how our path continues. Of course, some people have more difficulties and greater challenges. For them, the ability to walk onto a clearer path might take longer and involve more of a struggle.

Have you ever felt stuck in a pattern with certain family members and see no way to break free without hurting them or leaving them struggling? Do you have an adult child that you feel needs you or wouldn't be able to manage without your assistance? Every scenario holds a message if we have the courage and honesty to look at it from a broader perspective.

The world, and everyone in it, acts as a mirror to what we believe about ourselves and what we feel we deserve. Sometimes, other people may give us hints about the themes we must overcome and the effects of the choices we make. But, ultimately, we choose which messages we believe and act on. We choose the music we download to our playlist, as well as the tunes that we delete. This is the sentiment at the heart of my forever-favorite prayer, The Serenity Prayer. '*God grant me the serenity to accept the things I cannot change, the courage to change the things I can, and the wisdom to know the difference.*' All the messages and answers lie in this prayer.

Every trial, setback, disappointment, or failure, falls into one of two categories: it's either something beyond our control or something that we can strive to change. Peace of mind and fulfillment in this life often come down to knowing the difference between the two and accepting the lesson that each of these scenarios can teach. It can be especially difficult to distinguish between the two categories when dealing with people we love. We can try to help someone, but we might be delaying their opportunity to learn a lesson and move on. Every individual must learn to say, "It is *my* responsibility to wake up, continue to ask the right questions, and listen to the hard, sometimes hurtful answers in each difficult situation I face."

I ask God to help me learn each lesson with the least amount of pain and that the lesson be complete, so it doesn't need to return. Setting this simple intention has eased tremendously the burdens I bear, allowing me to learn my lessons through insight rather than heartbreak. The goal in life is not to *not* have another setback but, rather, to build your life on sustaining principles, beliefs, skills, and approaches that can help you deal with anything that comes your way. With the help of my Higher Power—and, one step at a time—I can feel safe, confident, and alert.

The lessons and messages we receive on this healing journey help us progress through life in any number of ways. As we step beyond the tendency to use willpower to force and push ahead toward our goals, we can rely on our spiritual messages to provide feelings of peace, purpose, and passion. But, what happens when someone tries to move forward in life without hearing the messages or taking responsibility for their actions? Can you be truly successful if you don't take the opportunities to grow?

Most of us can recall a situation in our lives, or someone else's, where we forged ahead heedlessly, on the strength of willpower and persistence, to achieve the desired goal. However, before too long the goal that was so deeply desired had turned into a disaster, and we were left to pick up the pieces. This scenario is even more likely to happen when we feel vulnerable and start asking other people for direction without listening closely to ourselves and our guidance from God.

We must take the time to be silent and hear our small, quiet voice of wisdom. This takes courage because we may have to accept that we made a mistake or we need to retrace some steps. However, the longer it takes to listen, the larger the losses and the bigger the lesson becomes.

I remember a difficult time in my family when my husband wasn't working. After several months of being unemployed, he received a job offer in California. Despite strong reservations on my part, we made the joint decision to leave the New York City area and move out west. It was an enormous job to pack up and sell the house. The kids were young, which added to the challenge. It took six months of hard work, but we finally got all our plans in place. We were under contract to sell our house and purchase a new one on the West Coast. The old house was packed up, the moving van was scheduled, and I'd hired a crew to help us. Then, my husband's job fell through.

This happened during the Silicon Valley dot-com crash. Just like that, the company had been sold, and his offer was off the table. Looking back, I can only wish I would've listened to my inner guidance and dared to investigate the option of staying in our home. This would have meant backing out on our house sale and unpacking every box. I later learned that you can get out of a house sale even if it's tricky and difficult. But, instead, we forged ahead with the move and ended up facing many daunting challenges in the months ahead. In hindsight, I can't exactly say that it all was a mistake, even though several aspects of it felt that way. However, I did learn an enormous number of lessons.

Eventually, I found "my people" in California and was able to make lots of friends. I became a part of the sound healing world, even as I continued a rich life in the classical performing and teaching scene. My kids also made many friends and had valuable experiences. Ultimately, we were able to turn the situation around and make the best of it. To this day, I can see the many ways we would've prospered financially if we'd heeded the intuition that led me to want to stay on the East Coast. But, maybe we would have lost so many of the lessons that we needed as our lives and challenges continued. This experience showed me that valuable lessons can come to you, no matter what you decide to do. It's just that most of us would rather not have to do it the "hard way."

When people refuse to honor their lessons, they often stay stuck in denial, which is a tough place to be. Unfortunately, negative subconscious patterns are very difficult, almost impossible, for the individual to notice for themselves, even while the message is painfully loud for anyone around them. It takes a lot of focused intention as you ask God to tune up the volume of awareness, and possibly allow you to hear gentle feedback from others. The usual tendency, because we can't see what we're doing, is to get defensive; after all, we have a lot invested in staying the way we know so well. You can probably look at some reoccurring painful situations in your life that might have had, or still have, an element of hanging onto old patterns; if you stay in denial, things get progressively worse. Each time the same lesson needs to be repeated, the dynamics and consequences become more difficult. This is our Higher Power's way of trying to get our attention. Denial is linked to fear. If you realize that you've been in denial about a particular challenge, ask yourself: what are you afraid of facing? Why do you need to create and live in an illusion to feel safe while, in reality, you become more exposed? The answers to these questions will find their genesis somewhere in your core beliefs. Uncovering and changing these beliefs is the only way to live in the truth.

Denial is just one of the many coping mechanisms that people use to avoid self-reflection; being content with life as it *appears* to be may feel like the safer choice emotionally, even if that's far from the truth. Remember that our minds, and even sometimes our hearts, don't truly know the difference between what's real and what's imagined. We must use all of the tools we're learning to create new patterns—ones that are helpful and real.

Like denial, defensiveness is a coping mechanism that is meant to keep a person's vision of reality from being threatened. Many people become defensive whenever something pops up that could call their judgment or motives into question. No one wants to be wrong! Especially when life can already seem so unfair at times. We need God's grace to change this position to a softer, more accepting attitude. We mustn't get caught up in thoughts about right or wrong, good or bad, better or best. Instead, our focus must stay on lasting principles like empathy, compassion, and connection with others. There are few benefits to having a judgmental attitude, whereas the lessons you learn by striving for greater connection and understanding will help you gain lasting wisdom.

One of my favorite things about learning to improvise on the viola is the motto that there are "no wrong notes." I encourage you to adopt this motto as you listen and create new music for the soundtrack of your life's movie. Remember to be patient; we're all doing our best. Listen with the purpose of learning without judgment or criticism. For some, this might be a new approach. But, we'll never get the lessons life has undertaken to teach us if we don't try something new or allow ourselves to make a mistake. Defensiveness is a condition that thrives on the fear of being made wrong, and therefore, unacceptable to others.

Try to get comfortable with the idea that you can be seen as wrong in someone's eyes and still know that there's nothing fundamentally "wrong" with you. If you made an error in judgment, maybe you'll need to apologize and try something different next time. If you do something that you're unhappy with, take a step back and examine the situation as objectively as you can. Assess what could've been done better on your part and resolve to make those changes in the future. Then, let it go. The more loving we can be to ourselves, the more invitations we'll have to move away from destructive behaviors.

My son is a recovering drug addict. During his active addict days, he loved to find some way to blame me for something or cause any chaos to take the focus off him. Unfortunately, it was very effective in the sense that the important issues became lost in a cacophony of hurt feelings and accusations. But, this ploy wasn't ultimately effective because, over time, it simply highlighted more of the aspects that needed to, and eventually did, change.

When we're tempted to use negative behaviors to meet a need or achieve a goal, the person harmed in the interaction is always us. It adds one more dissonant note that keeps you out of tune and delays your ability to hear your song. Coping mechanisms aren't harmful by definition. They play an important role in our lives. They help us feel secure. They make us believe there's an easier way out of the tough and painful situations that we find ourselves in. They give us a way and place to hide. But, ultimately, they also prevent us from ever being able to reach our destination, which is healing and the emotional freedom that flourishes when we live whole-heartedly.

As I've mentioned before, healing happens, in part, for our protection. Imagine that, one day, every negative habit was removed from your life and every dream laid out before you as real. The average person would have no idea of who they are without the identifiers and protective mechanisms the ego provides. To be instantaneously free would be enormously frightening. We need to move forward steadily on our new path step by step, as we get more in touch with who we really are. As we heal, we start to express our authentic identity—the eternal truth of our being, which resides within the spirit and pre-dates any ego-driven ideas we have about ourselves. It also increases our level of personal responsibility by raising our conscious awareness of how our actions affect others and how we alone will be held accountable for shaping our life's path.

To heal and embrace change is an exhilarating experience. Most of the time, there will be a few rough patches getting to the other side of the healing. But, as the saying goes, no pain no gain. And, growth feels great! It provides the chance to integrate what you've learned before moving on to address the new challenges in another layer. This process also allows for the chance to develop newer, supportive habits as you apply what you've learned. Over time, this is how we begin to appreciate each layer of healing work as a new opportunity to enjoy life even more. So, let go of control. Surrender and watch as miracles happen, questions turn into answers, and things begin to fall into place.

Acceptance and belief are components crucial to this healing journey. We can undo all the good work we've done by doubting and questioning ourselves—behaviors that often lead to self-sabotage. Fear and faith don't co-exist. Doubt can mean that there are more negative core beliefs beneath the surface that need clearing, tuning, and shifting; each of us must accept and believe in the change we've received. Own the change, be the change, and that change will continue to reverberate throughout your life positively.

Another important concept to understand is the difference between the subconscious and conscious mind. Though the subconscious rules our belief system, we do need the conscious mind to agree with our goals. The conscious mind can open the door and direct the changes that we are requesting. The conscious mind can also call upon our Higher Power and ask for help surrendering and allowing.

Because of the limitations of the conscious mind, I believe that our Higher Power gives us the grace to bypass the conscious mind after it's done directing us to the healing. Then, God can guide the changes in the subconscious mind. Studies have shown that this level of change includes shifts in our DNA. This is possible using the vibrating strings that connect us to Creation and All that Is. I find that before doing any healing exercise, it's most beneficial to ask for our Higher Power's help in directing our path. We need to guide our thoughts to an almost dream-like state where the conscious mind no longer needs to be in charge.

To achieve this state, sit comfortably and take some deep breaths. Ask your Higher Power to help you release and connect to Divine energy. Then, imagine yourself as a ball of energy. See that energy expand and move above your head. Keep moving through the ceiling, the building, through the clouds, through the outer reaches of the atmosphere, through the stars, and keep moving until you feel connected to the highest place you can fathom. You may feel energy moving in your eyes, or you may sense a white light. It will be different for everyone. But, the point is to bask in the energy of unconditional love and connection that binds the universe together. Remember, this is not something to overthink. Feel it, don't analyze it. Then, ask your Higher Power to assist with all your requests, including tapping into a core belief. We can ask our Higher Power to assist us in letting go of the negative core belief that no longer serves us.

We can also use a process that's similar to downloading information from the internet onto our phones. We ask our Higher Power to download and install a new, positive belief to replace the negative core belief that has been removed. Our Higher Power can dream so much bigger than we can imagine! That's why it's best not to try to direct the "how" when we ask for what we want. God is capable of creating avenues for answered prayer to manifest in our lives that are beyond the mind's ability to understand or anticipate. Trying to predict or force "how" it happens will make it so much more difficult for the dream to evolve and manifest. Besides, we can't put limitations on the infinite. Instead, we must seek to work in concert with the perfectly orchestrated harmony of God.

The tune-up practice enables us to build the strength to face our most challenging problems and situations. It teaches us to listen and live in the heart. Any form of pausing and listening to any sound around you will help to fine-tune your ability to hear what's going on. Intention setting, and active listening produce an environment of safety and openness, which is conducive to hearing the truth.

Part of this change has to do with practice. It takes time and lots of repetition to form the new pathways. Eventually, they'll become the new default setting. But, until then, it takes determination, effort, and action, to anchor the desire for change. Remember to be patient and kind. Applaud yourself for your progress whenever you can. As they say, it's progress, not perfection. It's the journey, not the destination. Life gives us so many chances, so many choices. Choose the best because you are worth it!

Tuning up provides a chance to hear the still, quiet voice within. The voice of truth, of our Higher Power, is quiet and gentle. It doesn't give us demanding orders. Rather, there's a high vibration of love that knows our purpose, that's waiting for us to ask for help finding and staying on this path. Tune in and ask yourself; what emotions you are feeling? Are you calm or stressed? Is your face relaxed? How is your breathing? Right now, take a deep breath in through your nose, hold your breath, and then exhale through your mouth releasing a sound. Feel the tension release from your eyes, cheeks, and mouth. Repeat this breathing exercise until you begin to feel relaxed and attuned to the quiet voice of the Divine.

Regular use of these kinds of easy and effective practices provide the opportunity to face our negative emotions, like denial, anger or avoidance, while still choosing healthier actions. One of my favorite parts of this process is when we're able to pause and watch our minds choose and reinforce the healthier, positive pathway. There are many exercises that will take the healing quest to the deepest levels of our being, bypassing our subconscious denial and other coping strategies.

One such exercise is something I call, "Unraveling the Answers".

Begin meditating by using the breathing exercise above. Then, ask for guidance to understand more about how negative coping mechanisms like denial and avoidance might be showing up in your life. Bring to mind what is bothering you. If your mind is at peace, move to the following step.

Bring in a strong image of the feelings that are painful, stressful, disturbing, and causing distress and feel them. Ask for guidance with questions like:

- How do you believe they help you get through difficult challenges?

- Do they feel helpful at the moment, only for you to discover later on that there's a much higher cost than anticipated?

- Are you taking care of your needs?

- Which ones could you improve on?

Imagine reenacting this unhelpful coping strategy using a drum. Take a deep breath and then play these feelings on your drum. Release through the rhythm, the pounding, feel the release. Without analyzing and thinking, at this moment, feel the pain and the release. As you release, think of what music goes as a soundtrack beneath this scene in your life and how can you change the music.

Imagine, and feel yourself moving into positive behaviors that will replace it. Get up and move, dance, feel the changes in your body, how you move freely, with confidence. The key is to acknowledge and thank whatever pattern has served you until now and give it permission to leave you. Watch and listen to the dissonance; adjust and tune as the discordant notes fall away and leave beautiful harmonies.

Now you can continue to create beautiful melodies on top of these stable new harmonic patterns of support. We can use drums and dance to help us process some of our negative, blocking feelings; the ones that are ready to release resolve into a transformation, and celebration.

Imagine how it will feel when the situations are resolved, when things are changed so that you feel good, you are empowered and grateful. Now, live in the reality of how that scenario feels as it "happens" now, in the moment. End with a symbolic rhythmical affirmation of gratitude as simple as, "thank you, thank you, thank you, it is done."

Repeat these steps with each disturbing situation and thought.

As was just suggested, it is important to include movement along with these exercises. A fun exercise you can do involves gathering a group of people together for a little dance party. Or, you can try it by putting on some of your favorite dance tunes. Divide your group into two sections, with one-half drumming and the other half dancing. Invite the dancers to connect to their bodies through the rhythm of the drums. Listen and move without over-thinking or judging the movements. The most important thing is to move freely. Change the rhythms to match different emotions such as chaos, anger, being stuck, depressed, peaceful, flowing, joyful, etc. Ask the dancers to set the intention to allow energy to flow through them as their bodies release any stored pain and hurt feelings in the body and then explode with new found freedom. After a while, switch places so the drummers can dance while the first group of dancers creates the music for the various soundtracks.

A different version of the above exercise includes and is based upon creating different playlists, pre-recorded soundtracks for what you feel ready to process, music that evokes different moods that will call forth different memories and times from your past, as well as music to applaud and reinforce new ways and endless possibilities. Begin by connecting with your Higher Power, which is important for all of the exercises. Move from meditating and listen for messages and themes, to free-flow writing and tearing up the paper, to chanting and drumming, and then move it through your body and end with a celebratory dance to integrate the re-wiring of new subconscious programs. Remember that the ongoing tune-ups and self-care keep you in alignment and harmony.

Staying in tune with our Higher Power keeps us on track when life events—or our own false beliefs—try to pull us off our chosen path. I once was called on to do healing work for a woman who weighed only 85 pounds. When I first saw Lucille, I was shocked by her condition. She looked terrible and suffered from many ailments including psoriasis. Lucille believed that she was dying, and this appeared to be the case. She was bleeding internally and ate a diet restricted to only two or three items. She was a very eccentric and spiritual person, and she followed this diet with great conviction and certainty. Lucille believed that if she ate anything else, she would die almost immediately. Despite seeing various doctors and healers over the years, she hadn't found answers to her condition.

As I continued to do vibrational healing energy work to remove and tune up deep subconscious programming, she gradually improved. Finally, one day I realized that she had an eating disorder caused by emotional blocks that originated in some damaging subconscious core beliefs. Her internal bleeding and weight problems weren't a manifestation of some mysterious illness, which doctors believed, but instead, it was caused by her belief that the strict diet was what was keeping her alive. The illness was, in fact, being caused by the diet.

As we worked through many core beliefs that held these unhelpful patterns in place, Lucille gradually, by the grace of God, became strong and healthy. She began eating a healthy diet filled with nutrient-rich, whole foods and was finally able to lead a full life. Lucille's mind, body, and spirit had come into alignment, and she could sing her "tune" freely. This was an extreme case, but it's an example of how negative subconscious core beliefs can stop us from living fully. Even actions that we believe are based on our desire to heal and recover can, in reality, be inflicting further damage.

I remember helping a young woman named Sara, who was married with three very young children. She ran an at-home business. Sara had an effervescent personality, but was plagued with severe fibromyalgia, which left her exhausted, in pain, and confined to her bed, often twice a week, sometimes more. Of course, this made many things in her life extremely difficult. We worked on shifting core beliefs about her value, her worth, and beliefs about love before we even began to talk about what might be wrong with her physical body.

We listened closely for whatever musical themes were running beneath what otherwise appeared to be a "nice melody." Some of her core beliefs involved concerns that she could never get her work done, she was never good enough to complete things, she needed to earn love, and life was difficult. Her beliefs were replaced with asking her Higher Power to teach her that she knows how to rest and have enough energy and she knows how to receive love. After a week or two, she was able to get through her weeks filled with energy.

This is an example of the power of God's grace and faith as we are open to learning and receiving. Sometimes, this awareness comes as an "aha moment", what Dr. Lipton calls "super learning." And, I prefer to call it a miracle. Other times, a miracle built on new awarenesses can come over a period of time. While you read this, please don't sit back and think, *wow, isn't that nice for her, but something like this couldn't ever happen to me.* If that thought crosses your mind, ask yourself, *well, why not?* Why not you? The only requirement is the desire, openness, and commitment to feel better. If you feel that this is too far-fetched, or too weird, might you instead really feel like you aren't worthy of a miracle?

As we learn to listen, tune-up, and align, we can be spared a lot of unforeseen hardships that would otherwise remain unknown. But, we must listen more deeply and be willing to change. Even when the unexpected happens, we won't be caught off guard as much, and most importantly, we'll have the tools to work through the challenges more easily. In this way, life can feel more stable, safer, and less stressful.

SIX
FINDING HARMONY

Personal harmony enriches our relationships in the same way that musical harmony enhances a song. In relationships, we practice the interplay of our "notes," creating the acceptance and connection that we all so desperately crave. Having poor relationships leaves us feeling empty, as if we were trying to play each of the parts of a symphony separately, rather than as an intricate and simultaneously occurring interchange of sound.

We can't have healthy relationships unless we're strong and whole within ourselves. If we are not firmly rooted in our personal wellbeing, we invariably get stuck in an impossible search for another person to make us whole and fill in our missing notes. But, that person doesn't exist. And, the search for that person can only lead us toward unhealthy, co-dependent relationships, in which the partners put aside their own wellbeing to maintain a relationship.

Healthy relationships thrive on balance, or interdependence, in which two strong individuals are involved and supportive of each other, but do not sacrifice themselves or compromise their values. Interdependency is one of the keys to having peace, harmony, and a life based on love. It's ironic that to be successfully interdependent, we must first be independent and whole within ourselves. Otherwise, it's like we're trying to sing our unique, resonant pitch with the mute button on. No one can hear us, and we cannot hear ourselves.

When we're not heard, harmony isn't possible. In that case, we can hear the other person's note, but we aren't present in the relationship; we're just hiding in it, and our beautiful notes cannot harmonize. When we agree, even tacitly, to remain silent and invisible, the dynamic exacerbates the belief that we aren't enough. Over time, the pattern created by this core belief leaves us feeling unsafe and usually disappointed in relationships. The connection we seek moves further away from us with each new layer of pain wrapped around our heart. Each layer hides our true self even more.

This pattern also re-affirms the false idea that a less dominant person is somehow not as valuable as those who speak and act boldly on their behalf. Releasing these false beliefs provides the space to engage in healthy, interdependent relationships. This creates the highest level of harmony and meaning in our lives. Sharing with others from this place of truth increases what we have by ten-fold because we're resonating with our authentic self.

Resonance, you recall, is a phenomenon in which a vibrating system or external force drives another system to vibrate at a specific frequency. Take the strings on a viola. I can put my finger on a lower string, creating the pitch A, and the corresponding open string will begin to vibrate. You can hear that note "humming" along. Or, when I play a note, say a 3rd finger G, the open G string an octave lower will begin to vibrate, activated as part of the overtones.

To put this concept in perspective, think of your torso as the body of a viola. The air around you is like the bow activating the strings of your viola and the folds in your vocal chords are like the bridge of the viola that passes the vibrations into the body of your instrument, which is then released through the f-holes, those curlicue holes cut into the front of the instrument.

Your instrument, your body, is tuned to a particular pitch, as are the spaces you inhabit. Other people can sense the sound emanating from you—your frequency. If you are not tuning into or aligning with your resonant pitch, your unique "in-tune" voice is muted. How can you resonate interdependently with another person? When your pitch is muted, the other person's resonant pitch reverberates in place of your own.

We must activate and tune our resonant pitch before we can ever hope to achieve harmony and interdependence in relationships. The interaction of our supportive "notes" creates richness, interest, and structure; without it, the notes are random and rather meaningless. Singular notes create isolated pitches, whereas notes created within a composition provide purpose and context. Resonant interactions and communication with others support interdependency, enhance our lives, and invite us to step into our full potential.

Relationships tend to be our main teachers. The people around us mirror our thoughts and beliefs. If we're unable to look at each relationship, whether good or bad, and ask God to reveal our part in any disharmony that's been created, we'll remain stuck in the negative energy we want to avoid. We'll continue to play the role of the victim and in that dynamic, we magnetically attract more pain. We have a choice to be a victim or not. If we choose to empower ourselves, we can count on God's grace to help us begin to understand our unhealthy patterns and to reveal, remove, and replace, the learned core beliefs that created them.

If we could somehow live in isolation, without relationships, not only would we be lonely, but we'd have fewer opportunities to grow and share the most wonderful parts of ourselves. Some people, who've been hurt very deeply and don't understand the possibility to heal, choose to be isolated. It reminds me of the parable of talents in Matthew 25: 14-30. Three men are asked to be stewards of different amounts of money. The first two were given the most amount of money; they trusted God and used the money and multiplied it. The third steward was given the smallest amount. Out of fear and misunderstanding of his role, he buried the money, thinking he was keeping it safe. But, he never received the benefits or rewards.

Of course, the money in this parable represents the talents and gifts we're given when we enter this world. I believe that having the courage to be fully engaged in relationships, asking for guidance, and tuning in and tuning up increases the gifts we receive in life. In being aligned with God, and connected to Mother Earth, we are better able to hear and find the ensemble of "our people" who were meant to resonate with us at our unique pitch.

But, though our ability to connect with each other is crucial, intimate relationships can be difficult and fraught with pitfalls. To be successful, we need to let other people into vulnerable places that might have experienced hurt in the past. Lingering hurts are connected to negative core beliefs, which usually create a series of experiences as they play themselves out in any number of scenarios; we're always hoping for a different ending that never happens. Some people have little-unhealed pain, and they feel safe being real and open. However, other people have a history of emotional lack or neglect to contend with. When we're not accustomed to experiencing unconditional love, we fall into the traps set by our subconscious patterns.

The pain gets deeper each time we fall into a trap. Then, we become more afraid and show even less of who we are as a way to protect ourselves. But, when that happens, the other person is loving an image rather than who we really are. This creates more distance and the fear of not being loved and accepted enough. The disconnections lead to misunderstandings, which is unavoidable because the relationship is built on a faulty premise. The list of ways this can play out is endless, but none of them have happy endings. The biggest pitfall is fear—being afraid of being seen, not being enough, or being abandoned by someone we love.

When I was a child, I experienced instances of separation from my caregivers that showed a deep-seated fear of abandonment. When I was two years old, my family was in the middle of a move from Vancouver, British Columbia, back to the U.S. The house had been cleared out, and the moving van had left. That evening, my parents left my brother and me with friends while they went off to a gathering. This was all normal, except, that while they were gone, I somehow got out of the house and wandered onto a very busy road. The police found me standing all alone on the divider separating many lanes of traffic. My parents didn't know this had happened until the next morning when they woke up to find me saying, "found mommy" and they heard from my five-year-old brother about my near miss.

Another time, when I was about five, I got lost on a huge beach in Chicago. I'd gone to the bathroom with some older girls, and we became separated. I remember looking at the sea of hundreds of faces and wondering how I would ever find my parents and get home. Once again, the police helped me find my family.

Over the years, when these stories came up, they were told with a light-hearted spin that made everyone laugh, including me. It took me decades to realize that the pain of these experiences was real, that I felt unsafe, and maybe even endangered. I'd been fundamentally affected by these frightening experiences, and they created subconscious core beliefs about myself and life. It took a lot of work—this work I'm sharing with you—to bring these beliefs to light and shift them.

Now, I can be grateful because these experiences were part of what led me to spend so much of my time seeking spiritual guidance, safety, and protection, even from a very young age. I developed a strong connection with God, which has given me more faith and access to many miracles. What I once felt as a lack—based on my experiences translated into my inadequacies—is now "filled in" with God's grace, understanding, and love.

Our most crucial and fundamental relationship is with our parents. In a sense, they represent God to us, an omnipotent force that we are one hundred percent dependent upon for the fulfillment of all of our needs. Our parents teach us our worth. Through them, we learn to experience and express love. We learn if our needs will be understood and met and how much we're worthy of receiving. This relationship creates and embeds our core beliefs as the dynamics of this relationship are experienced over and over with each passing hour during our infancy and childhood.

As we grow, we take what we've learned and step out on our own to sink or swim. Is the world a safe place? Do we know how to make wise, healthy choices? As children, were we encouraged or were we constantly criticized and berated? Did we engage in a competition with a parent and experience sabotage instead of support? With the coming of adulthood, we must choose whether to repeat our core lessons or use new tools to reset our core beliefs.

Despite the challenges that I experienced, I have a deep gratitude for my parents and every effort and gift they gave me. I have been given grace from God to go beneath all the details and day-to-day experiences and to connect with their complete love beneath it all. I now know they did the very best that they could, based on what they had been taught as children. My parents played their "role" perfectly, and I can now claim all of the love I wasn't able to feel then.

Obviously, a child's personality influences the way their formative relationships affect them. But, generally, after the first seven years, we have formed the relationship with our self. As a result of our earliest interactions, the messages we've been told, about who we are and what we deserve, will dictate how we will apply the mental, emotional, spiritual, and physical relationship to our own existence.

For me, being very sensitive and spiritually minded, the effect was huge. Even my desire to play music was, in my mind, met with disapproval. When my public orchestra teacher noticed some talent and suggested to my parent's that I take viola lessons, they feared that it would be a wasted expense and a repeat of the piano lessons for which I often did not prepare. I determined I would take viola lessons and continue forging ahead no matter the obstacles. Thankfully, we found a viola teacher in the Minnesota Orchestra who lived in our area.

I loved playing the viola, and signs of success began showing up immediately. My parents weren't always excited and supportive; this was a world they didn't know. For them, my lessons were a pricey "extra" activity. I devised ways to help pay for my music. I was a popular babysitter after all the experience I had with my baby sister. I saved all of my babysitting money and bought my first real viola, enough to make it happen. I remember how resourceful I felt and proud I was! I can remember, like it was yesterday, everything about buying and playing it.

More lessons and summer camps and world travel followed, all driven by my ambition and initiative. My determination to play, and the subsequent appearance of a teacher and a viola in my life, demonstrated to me that I could control my destiny.

But, along with the victories and success came hardships. I seemed to find teachers who took on familiar, disapproving roles. I often felt stuck in a cycle of being misunderstood and feeling unsupported and abandoned. I searched for a mentor and trusted confidant—one who would go to bat for me, prepare me, and open up my opportunities. Except that didn't happen.

My rocky road didn't start to smooth out until I stopped looking for that person and started being that person. Looking back, I can now see how experiences were based on my subconscious programming. My gifts of music and faith have always helped me to move forward, even when faced with challenges. For many years, I explored the connection between faith, music, joy, happiness, and struggles. I now believe that it is in the connections that we find the answers.

As I was discovering who I was, music helped to make that connection. As I developed the SoundPath techniques, I realized that even though everyone doesn't necessarily own and know how to play the viola, everyone is a drummer and drums are everywhere, even inside of us. I love to use drums and percussion instruments, bells, shakers, tambourines, wood blocks, etc., in SoundPath work because they are non-verbal and can directly communicate with the subconscious mind. Each drum brings its boundaries and offers unique possibilities when exploring connections.

One of my favorite activities you can easily do in a group or individually. When I offer this activity in a workshop, I let everyone choose a drum, and I ask them to close their eyes and imagine that they are sitting in a circle in an African village, and the drum is to be used to communicate. I ask the participants to focus on what they are feeling. Sometimes, I ask particular questions to guide them such as: "What is the hardest thing for you to do and why?" "How does it feel to cry?" "What was the last thing or who was the last person that made you angry?" "How does it feel to be out-of-sorts, out-of-tune, out-of-control?" I ask them to express their feelings directly through the drum without any analytical thoughts—let the drum do the communicating for them. At the end of the drumming—everyone seems to know intuitively when to end—the group sits in silence and listens to the rhythms within. Each time, magic and transformations happen where it matters the most, in the heart.

When I have presented this program at alcohol and drug rehabs, I have seen the most resistant and angry person, at first unwilling to participate, transform into the most excited participant who only wants to do it more often. The group offers stability and a safe place to belong and express themselves.

Today, I am still learning how important it is to take care of myself first. I think of the analogy-cum-adage that you first need to put the oxygen mask on yourself before you put it on anyone else. It took work for me to realize that I'm not selfish when I take care of myself. It doesn't mean that I don't care about my kids or other family members as much as myself. But, if I put the proverbial oxygen mask on them and not on myself in time, I could die and not be there to help anyone at all.

For me, learning about self-love, self-respect, acceptance, and healthy boundaries, was a struggle because of the experiences ingrained in my subconscious patterns. It was imperative that I learn to tune myself up regularly, to get back into alignment with what's true and most important about myself. Then, I could give to others from the overflow of my love and concern, rather than giving until it depleted me. I had to learn to set boundaries and say the powerful, not-always-liked word "no."

Boundaries help both parties to stand in their truth. In a recording studio, if there aren't any barriers between the musicians, the sounds are all blended, and it isn't possible to edit individual parts or to find balance between the separate parts. If another person's volume is too loud, you can't hear what you're playing. And, if they're playing in an intense, egotistical way, there isn't room to add your own voice.

Balance and boundaries provide us with the freedom to improvise. In music, as in life, the ability to improvise allows me to connect to God and play what comes, as if I'm dialed into a channel that magnifies God's music through me. It's a powerful process of complete faith. If I have doubt or fear about how it might sound, I am instantaneously cut off from the flow.

Besides our parents and early caregivers, the other most intense relationships that we're likely to experience are between ourselves and close relatives, like siblings and children. For many people, their relationship with their spouse or partner falls into this category of lifelong bonds that shape who they are and how they view the world. Our closest relationships are like magnifying glasses or microphones amplifying our core beliefs and activating our lessons.

When we have unresolved issues, there's bound to be more strife in our relationships unless we choose to disengage or only partially reveal ourselves. But, these strategies are half-measures that carry their own risks as well. Working through any triggers in familial relationships helps us get closer to connecting with and resolving our core beliefs. Our relationships assume more meaning as we delve into our lessons on giving and receiving.

People with siblings are influenced by the bond in unique ways. Many factors affect how we interact with siblings separately and together, including birth order, and how our parents treated our siblings—especially if it was very different from how we were treated. While favoritism in families is incredibly common, it's extremely damaging for the favorite child and the outcast, albeit in different ways.

It's amazing how aspects of these childhood relationships affect us throughout our lives. I remember a social worker at a health care facility telling me that when a parent is sick and nearing the end of life, it brings out the worst in everyone. All the childhood roles are played out to an extreme. I didn't believe that was possible until I experienced some of this during my father's battle with Parkinson's disease and his death. Everyone struggled in their own way. I noticed that because of my experience and interpretation of my brother and sister being treated differently from me, it added to my feeling of being less-than and the need to seek external validation of my worth. But, as part of my tune-up process, I had to re-examine all the old expectations and belief systems that had contributed to any pre-conceived notions about my self-worth and identity.

Having a sibling can be a gift of companionship, unconditional love, and someone to walk through life with who knows you in a way no one else ever will. I am very grateful for my siblings. But, these relationships must be maintained in a healthy way. They must mature to stay vibrant and alive. Holding onto old roles not only damages the sibling relationship, it stunts individual growth. Even when we have ideas that appear to be positive on the surface (I was the smart one; I was the athletic one; I was the black sheep; I was the star; I was the pretty one) it can be detrimental if those beliefs become confining. When a person is afraid to change or make mistakes, vital parts of his or her personality start to atrophy.

Choosing to become a parent requires us to grow in ways that we may never have expected. Parenting has been one of my biggest teachers. I'd always wanted to be a mom, more than anything. I spent years of my adult life going to therapy and learning many healing modalities to prepare myself. I always wanted to be the best person and mom that I could be. Over the years, I was faced with many struggles and challenges; I could have easily considered myself a colossal failure, and sometimes I did. But, overall, I have always known that I loved my kids more than anything, and I did my best. I set out to change the relationship dynamic

I experienced with my parents, hoping to instill a somewhat different set of beliefs in my children.

Now, I have the joy of seeing my daughter and son doing fabulously well and in beautiful relationships. I know this is mainly because of God's grace, my fervent prayers, commitment, and the sincere love that was always underneath everything I did—and even what I wasn't able to do. It's never been an easy journey. Knowing when to step back and allow one's children to cope with life's hardships on their own is tough. It's a fine line I didn't always see. But, embracing the challenge gave me the opportunity to ask my Higher Power for guidance.

As a parent, and at that time, it was difficult for me to realize how different my kids' temperament and needs were. There are many things that I wish I could have done differently, and better and yet, I am thankful for all that I have been able to do.

My daughter was very independent and kind of tough. She had a few "mean girl" challenges growing up, but she let things take their course, and eventually, those situations made her stronger. She was beautiful, outgoing, a leader among her peer group, intelligent, gifted, she worked very hard, and she was lots of fun to be with. We had our differences, and we weren't always very close, especially during her teenage years. But, things worked out. I pushed her hard to have jobs and be a leader. She is happy, extremely successful, and enjoying life fully!

My son was considerate, personable, very sensitive and amazingly gifted in so many special ways. He was so cute, exceptionally smart, had a huge sense of humor, and was lots of fun. My son has his own story to share. We have discussed how we both want to share our experience, strength, and hope with the intention of helping others. He generously allows me to share that he struggled with anxiety and depression throughout his high school years. This led to multiple suicide attempts and a flourishing drug addiction. Thankfully, after multiple rehabs, immense faith, and the support of loved ones, he is successfully completing college and living a fantastic life drug-free and happy.

One of my most significant memories and lessons as my son's mom was the time that I was at the Omega Institute workshop featuring an international healer who has been recognized in the media, including two Oprah Winfrey shows. God has used this healer to help many people from around the world receive miraculous healing, often several thousand people a day. While there, I received a message that my son was struggling for his life. Unable to find clear cell service and finding myself unable to travel fast enough to be with him, my only choice was to pray in the most intense way possible. I focused on seeing my son doing well. As my son has shared, he was aware that his body functions were shutting down and he could see the end of his life nearby, a thought came into his head that he would be okay, and he just needed to push through it. My son acknowledges that this was God's voice that came to him, at that moment, it was a thought that just wasn't his own. By God's grace, he had the courage to surrender to the voice, take action, and move forward. For me, this is the clearest example, and lesson, that the most that we can do for our loved ones, and anyone we want to help, is to pray for them. We also need to pray for ourselves so that we can listen, remain strong and connected to the highest energy with faith, and take the best action steps, one moment at a time. At that particular moment, I needed to generate and be the qualities that I wanted for my son to have for himself. I am most grateful to both of my children for the lessons they have taught me, and there are more for me to learn.

As parents, our actions speak louder than words. Forgiveness, gratitude, and positivity go a long way toward creating the space for our children to see and know the best about themselves. So, always do your best to see your children doing great things, no matter how different circumstances may look at the moment. And, always do the same for yourself. Take a pause, listen, tune in, and tune up, so that you can stand in alignment with your truth and resonate with the beauty of your song.

The people we love want us to be operating at our best. This is true of our relationships with our children, and it's equally true in our romantic relationships. Our spouse or significant other is a perfect mirror for us. These relationships will bring out the absolute best parts of who we are—the kindness, the generosity, the spontaneity, the passion, and the joy. But, they also set the stage for our negative core beliefs to show up, staring us in the face—if we can see them.

Relationships show us how we're able to give and receive love, to accept someone else's faults fully, along with our own. To keep our relationships healthy and vital, we must ask ourselves questions like: How do I impact my partner? Which patterns in this relationship are healthy, and which patterns continue to create struggles? Do I set unrealistic expectations for my partner, based on some outcome I think I can control—even when it involves someone else who has free will? Do I expect my partner to read my mind instead of stating my needs in a clear and forthright way? What are my boundaries?

Every relationship starts with yourself. It's no one else's responsibility to "complete you" or save you from an unhappy life. We can't expect someone else to swoop in to make us feel whole. The understanding of being good enough can only come from within, with the help of God. When a person seeks a feeling of wholeness from another human being, it puts unsustainable pressure on the relationship.

A long-term relationship goes through a normal progression of stages. In the beginning is the "honeymoon stage", when we create an idealized picture of our beloved, without seeing or knowing about any of that person's faults. Later, in the relationship or marriage, when the faults start popping up, we can become frustrated and disappointed. What happened to our beautiful, easy-going partner? Many times, people give up at this point. But, if you make it through this adjustment period by focusing on yourself and how you can continue to bring your best self to the situation, you will eventually get to the point of rich understanding. Not only will you deepen your acceptance of your partner, but you'll be able to experience giving and receiving unconditional love.

Restoring harmony to our relationships means first being able to step back and look at our family members in a new way. It means knowing that we're separate from them and from any issues and differences that may have arisen in the past. Focus, instead, on connecting to your song and maintaining "good intonation," the term for when you play in tune. This clarity is what makes it possible to harmonize with the other person in the relationship.

Receiving my cancer diagnosis was my turning point that caused me to finally know that it was time to "put on my oxygen mask." My years of taking care of others, receiving negative treatment from others, giving without receiving—had to end. The person that needed to change was staring me in the face; this was my job. Even though I had the dream, and had been writing and discovering sound healing techniques for years now, I knew it was my turn and my time to draw a deep line in the sand and find ways to make these dreams a reality, a way of life.

As you stand in a place of alignment and peace, you can hold a space of high vibration and invite your loved one to join you in making positive changes. This takes a diligent commitment to being in alignment and being an expression of all that is good. We can accomplish this kind of real growth by letting go of the conscious mind as the "ruler" of our life circumstances. When we examine our core beliefs, an attitude of exploration will lead us to valuable discoveries.

This isn't about digging into your past to fixate on specific core beliefs, and it's certainly not about judging yourself for holding those beliefs. Rather, it's about finding the themes and feelings that created the core beliefs so that the result of the discovery process is release. Set the intention to let the conscious mind rest in the background. You can't solve a problem at the level of consciousness that helped to create it. So, while we use the conscious mind to guide and discover, we must open ourselves to the higher vibrational frequencies of surrender, trust, receiving, faith, and gratitude.

It helps to remember that our Higher Power is the creator of the vibrations, as well as the Source that guides the vibrations.

The energetic strings go to the hidden places within that need shifting, alignment, and balance. The strings use the process of entrainment, vibrating in harmony, adjusting until they find perfect alignment. With each vibrating breath, we can embrace harmony, joy, ease, and passion, as we resonate with our purpose.

Finding harmony within ourselves and our relationships helps to heal the heart. The heart is such a central part of our being, not just physically, but energetically and emotionally. How many times has your heart been broken, shocked, torn apart, beautifully touched, stretched, or badly bruised? How are you able to put the pieces back together when the experience has changed those pieces so that they no longer fit as perfectly as they once did?

Broken hearts need God's grace. Ask for help to find healing as you see and experience this vision: see your heart spinning counterclockwise and watch the unnecessary and hurtful debris become dislodged and thrown away. Now, envision the heart spinning clockwise as the parts you gave to others, those who didn't deserve it or treated you poorly, are called back—but only after God has first cleaned them and carefully, lovingly, released them to float back, integrated where they belong. Stay with this visualization as long as necessary, until you begin to feel the harmony and balance restored.

The heart is held by the soul, our spiritual fingerprint and ancient compass. However, there are those unfortunate people whose heart has been hardened by the pains and setbacks of life. They aren't able to be honest. They haven't gone through the process of being forgiven and forgiving, of being loving and accepting love. They've forgotten what it feels like to be truly grateful. For them, life is limited, lonely, and much more difficult than it needs to be. When the heart is hardened, it's almost impossible to create harmony with someone else.

Some people are born "tone deaf" and, in those rare instances, it's best not to try to sing with them. Instead, resolve to keep your harmony while accepting them as they are. Listen respectfully to whatever song they choose to sing, but know that their song doesn't have to harmonize with your song. Instead, focus on yourself and filling in any missing notes with love. Connect to the beauty of who you are and then share in the harmony that you create from that space of openness.

Our souls hold our unique and eternal imprint of all that we are. Remember that you're the seeker and the knower behind each lesson. And, your lessons are safe to learn because you are created and held with love. This is the place you resonate from, where your overtones are activated, and harmony is created. In this place, the heart finally can heal and be whole.

SEVEN
FINDING THE RIGHT TONE

Music is a window to my soul that connects me to spiritual realms. Music also connects me to other people, some whose faces I've never seen, and others whom I love but are no longer here on earth. Music has paved the way for me to travel around the world and have adventures beyond my wildest dreams. I feel very connected to my music; its rhythms are the same to me as my breath. It's an integral part of my soul that gives me hope and builds my faith. This unending journey with music has taught me so much. It provides a place where I feel "at home", a place where I experience my highest sense of purpose and belonging.

Most of us have wondered at some point, "where do I belong?" We all want to find the right pitch and tone quality. Musically speaking, a tone is subtle nuances and texture of the sound quality itself. The tone helps the clear pitch create a vibration that resonates with a certain mood, emotion, or message. Spiritually speaking, a tone can represent an aspect of the soul that resonates in full harmony with the people, places, and situations around us. It's also the level of vibratory frequency of our relationships. When we are in alignment, these are the "places" we can call home, where we feel loved and appreciated.

We all want to experience the feeling of being accepted and cherished just as we are. But, part of finding the right pitches and tone means engaging in reality-based assessments of our strengths and growth points. There are various modes and tools for making such assessments, including using music and vibration to help you tune up dissonance and chaos and find alignment. Music reflects the vibration that is resounding in your heart at the deepest level of your being; when you are in balance, you experience peace and clarity. Dissonance is resolved into harmony and beauty, which can resonate with all areas of your life.

Paying attention and using some of these exercises to tune-up our vibrational level brings clarity and positivity, that allows us to experience the connection to God, ourselves, and others that we crave. It allows us to initiate and communicate with a resonant pitch from within, similar to an in-tune pitch which activates overtones and is magnified when it is played.

Using vibrations to find alignment is also the basis of building spiritual and emotional clarity which allows us to see—and be—who we truly are. One of the most important things we can do is to allow ourselves to be authentic. Happiness and contentment will remain elusive as long as we remain disconnected from our authentic selves. This journey can be fun and life-affirming as we strive to find our tribe: the people who enjoy us just the way we are.

Growing up, I was very shy. I believed what I'd been told—that I needed to be seen and not heard. As a consequence, I felt a need to be quiet and take cover, which made it difficult to feel at ease and find where I fit. I felt comfortable once I found the viola and spent time with other musicians who became my tribe.

I started the viola quite late, and I felt I was at a deficit. Most kids began at an early age with lessons and frequent practice. I started in public middle school group lessons. Combining all that with an ADD diagnosis and plenty of insecurities, I often worried about being inadequate, particularly when I was around highly trained musicians. Even when I accomplished extraordinary things, like being accepted into the top quartet at Juilliard for two years in a row, the nagging doubts persisted.

After receiving my degrees at Juilliard, I decided to pursue graduate studies at Yale, with a culture where students were expected to act as if they knew it all. I was worried that my peers saw me as stupid. Yet, somehow, I passed all my advanced exams and managed to do quite well. I even exceeded the language requirement on a doctoral placement exam based on a knowledge of French that I learned in high school.

But, rather than viewing myself as someone who belonged in these wonderful places I found myself in, I questioned myself at every turn. For many years, my viola was my best friend, and it might even be fair to say that I hid behind the viola. The instrument was my voice. For me, the path to self-acceptance came through my dedication, passion, and all the lessons I learned through music. But, that path to understanding and accepting yourself is different for everyone, and, hopefully, the SoundPath techniques can help you find yours.

God created you with unique potential and purpose. If we walk a path that's not our own, we stop resonating with that purpose. Inevitably, we start harmonizing and blending into the supporting role of someone else's tune. This blocks our ability to explore the nuances of our genuine self and to find the courage to tune in, tune up, and sing our song with confidence and beauty. While our sense of authenticity is one of the most important things we can possess, one of the great paradoxes of modern life is that many people become invested in playing roles and wearing whatever mask they believe will allow them to fit in.

It's like being a kid at Halloween. When I was a child, I loved thinking about what character I was going to be that day. As an adult, it's quite an interesting exercise to ask yourself the same question: What character do you dress up as? What masks do you wear and why? Do you play a bold, aggressive character to give you more courage? Are you a "cool" character who is part of a trendy scene with other popular people? Are you a scary character who gets a feeling of confidence from having the power to control others and how they feel? Do you try to play an angelic character even when you feel like there's more than a little bit of devil inside?

When we get in touch with our authentic self, we stop playing those roles and anchor ourselves in reality. Other people can feel the power in our presence because we're resonating with what's true. A group of people vibrating on the same "wavelength" creates harmony and resonance felt by everyone who comes into contact with that frequency. The simultaneous connection is a type of entrainment. Of course, if you're in a group filled with bickering and strife, where everyone is speaking loudly and out of tune, the combined dissonance is magnified. There's great chaos, like horns honking in gridlocked traffic at a busy intersection. Everyone is out of sync and going nowhere.

We all want to find the right tone, that place in our lives where we feel completely accepted and free, where our purpose becomes clear, and we have the support to face our toughest challenges. In playing a musical instrument, the tone refers to the type and quality of the sound. Is it dark and rich, light and shimmering, does it have a raspy quality or a smooth and bright texture? A poor-quality tone might sound like someone scraping their nails on a chalkboard. But, finding the most fitting quality tone is very different than acquiescing to the desire to fit in. And, it's easy to mistake one for the other if we're not used to operating from a place of essential truth. Finding the right tone is finding a way to resonate fully with who we are and what we believe. It's discovering where we truly fit, not just where we fit in.

When people are confused and insecure, other voices may become more believable and meaningful than their own; they struggle to find an internal tone that adjusts and harmonizes with the din of those outside voices. Whenever we're tempted to fit in at all costs, we must slow down and remind ourselves to "do the next right thing." In this case, that means listening and connecting to your inner voice. Then, make a conscious effort to resonate with people and groups that magnify, blend, and harmonize with your authentic tone.

Imagine that we're always silently singing a song or playing a specific genre of music, in a particular key, that resonates with our moods, thoughts, and belief at any given time. When we are performing and sharing music authentically in alignment, people can feel the music that we're playing, and some will be drawn to join in energetically. But, if we aren't in tune with ourselves, if we lack confidence or were told that what we do doesn't matter, then our silent song won't attract people who support us. If the song is too quiet, our singing doesn't activate any vibrations either. The few people who join us in our singing may want to take over the music and change everything about it. People with that kind of energy like to be in control. But, in that scenario, you're making music that doesn't resonate with you at all. It is someone else's song. So, the people who might hear your whispered echo may not truly resonate with you at all.

Before I was able to learn and use these principles, I was a perfect target for people to take advantage of me. It was incredible how many times this happened over the years. They say no one is a victim without their consent. But, I was an example of someone who had no idea of why negative things would happen to me. Every time I encountered these kinds of situations, it left me feeling even worse about myself. A common thread I can now see, is that I gave my power away, which, over time, left me feeling even more vulnerable and depleted. As I fell into my "less than" role, I allowed and created an illusion that ultimately elevated another person's status. I set up situations that gave these people even more ability to mistreat me and sabotage my efforts.

I'd been taught since I was very young that if anything went wrong, it was my fault. I was given, and, after a while, willingly took, all of the blame. Taking on the guilt, shame, and blame, became my designated and well-rehearsed role. Con artists and others trying to take advantage of me tapped into this energy. Changing these core beliefs and patterns took years. But, using the various SoundPath concepts and exercises shortens the learning process.

Each realization and healing has the potential to happen instantly, but repeated practice will reinforce, retrain, and retain the ongoing growth and freedom from negative patterns. The SoundPath method will enable you to work through some historic and karmic lessons with more ease and in less time. You'll be able to hear the disharmony much quicker, and you can get out of problematic situations before extensive damage has been done. When you are more positive, you resonate at a higher frequency, and the people that surround you also operate from a higher place as well. It is very uplifting to be around people who are inspired and inspiring.

Being around people who make you feel welcome and supported rather than judged is like singing in a room with excellent acoustics. Acoustics provide the right amount of echo and warmth around a sound. Just as the chemistry between the instrument and player creates a unique sound, when you add a reverberant room, concert hall or church, the formula sparkles with added beauty and richness. In the same way, loving relationships provide the right amount of support to bring out your song. No matter how beautiful the tone of your music, without the right acoustics it will be impossible to hear the full richness of your song.

To make positive changes, we need to step away from any attachment to pain and blame. Our current life circumstances are the clearest and loudest reality check about what has been going on in our thoughts. Thoughts and words carry vibrations; those frequencies are magnetic, and they contribute to what we experience. To up-level our experiences, we have to work on creating thoughts, behaviors, and practices that will support the changes we desire in an ongoing way.

If you're ever feeling out of sorts or out of tune, pause for a moment to find the right tone before moving forward with any further action. First, sit in a comfortable position and close your eyes. Feel your feet connected to the floor. Listen to the silence while you take a deep breath in through your nose. Then release a tone out loud, while tuning your focus into your body. You can start off by humming and then move into different vowel sounds.

Feel any areas where the sound feels "stuck," or dissonant. Let the vibrations loosen, adjust, and shift the dissonance into harmony. Feel them touch every nook and cranny inside of you. Imagine that the vibrations are a dust cloth, or even a powerful vacuum cleaner, dislodging and collecting old debris that's clogging or interfering with the resonance of the sound. Change to different vowel sounds (ooh, aah, eee, ohh, etc.) allowing each sound to resonate freely. As you move the shape of your mouth to different vowels, listen for overtones. Repeat this exercise for as long as you like. Continue breathing normally and open your eyes when you're ready.

The vibrations you generate doing exercises like this can connect you to your heart by developing an attunement to the internal vibrating strings. For me, my heart is the "switchboard" through which everything must pass. The source that enables the connection is God, and the soul holds the switchboard. Our bodies react to sound, remembering that vibration is at the core of our being, connecting us to all matter.

These exercises help us reach the subconscious mind, beyond language and explanation, to use "ultrasonic surgery" to dislodge old patterns. Only then can we fill the stuck and empty spaces with unconditional love from God and reconnect to the place we remember in our mother's womb where all our needs were met, when we were enough, and we knew that we were loved. We innately know that we are unique and special, we were born to fit in and be cared for. That knowing remains beneath any chaos, and it is always there to reconnect to. The soul knows and never forgets the truth of who we are and what we are here to do. This is the connection we are seeking; we can now hear its quiet voice.

Even for the times when we weren't able to receive this fully as a child, we can do it now. We can re-set to our pre-trauma state. Trauma doesn't have to be a huge event covered in the media. We can experience chronic trauma over time—constant put-downs, feeling unsupported, or being subjected to any behavior that made us feel unloved, not cherished, our essence ignored, or unaccepted by our "tribe."

When we tune-in, amplify and fine-tune our resonant pitch, our connection to our soul, it helps us to attract the types of relationships that we want. The concept of the resonant pitch ties into the string theory of the fundamental vibrating strand, since all matter, including man and animals, is made up of the vibrating strands. Everything is attuned to a pitch. When the vibrations are activated and travel through the air as waves, they bounce around the space, and a "pitch" is created. This pitch activates overtones and resonates in a very open, magnified way. Life is navigated sonically, similar to the dolphins' ability to "see" and communicate through their keen sense and use of sound and resonance.

The concept of resonant pitch is also how we can break through calcified thought patterns, habits, and beliefs at the core of the sub-conscious. We use resonant pitch to "blast apart" the negative core beliefs, similar to ultrasonic surgery for a kidney stone. After the energy has cut through what is unwanted, that space is filled with loving, positive, and supportive energy. Then, we can create new organic choices rather than give in to strict or judgmental demands from the conscious mind. This "vibrational ultrasonic surgery" disassembles the defense mechanism we've created. As they're recognized and released, we can live freely, responding to each situation as it arises without seeing it through the lens of our stored trauma.

Many years ago, in my early days as a professional musician, I began sharing my concepts of vibrational healing and conducting healings at a care facility in New York City. Because of its location on the upper west side of Manhattan, many famous musicians, actors, and writers came there. I played the viola at the bedside of a famous poet during her final hours. Even in her fragile state, she started creating the most profound and beautiful poetry about how she was a hollow vessel, and the music was vibrating through her bones, transmitting her connection and passageway to God. She was so peaceful and filled with deep gratitude for the music and life.

It was as if the sounds were massaging every aspect of her spirit and soothing her frail, eighty-pound body—no longer able to serve her in this life. As she lay curled up in her bed, I could see her bones. Bones are a perfect conductor of vibration. Also, humans are comprised of sixty to seventy percent water, and sound travels four times faster through water than air. Her frail body was the perfect conductor for the music that was coming through me as I stood playing for this beautiful soul. This profound and spiritual experience confirmed all my reasons for seeking every chance to share music in this way.

Everyone has such a connection to something. For those who haven't experienced it yet, the task is to stay open and receptive to your purpose. Following your passion should feel natural and easy, like breathing. It goes beyond practical thoughts and analysis. Allow your thoughts to guide your reality in the direction of your dreams, asking God to guide the path and open the doors. Use each breath, each day, to bring you more opportunities to share your light and your truth with others. This is why you are here.

When I worked at the Manhattan care facility, I was asked to visit a famous violist. When I walked through his door, we were both shocked to realize we already knew each other. He'd been a mentor, and he seemed very concerned about seeing me in such an unlikely place, as if all of his support of me had failed. He would've much rather heard that I had a position with a major orchestra or quartet. Undeterred, I played for him at his bedside. My old mentor was very moved. I was able to give back to him with love in the way that felt the most powerful to me.

The New York Times critics might not applaud me, but I no longer was seeking this type of success, recognition, or approval. I didn't fit into the norm for a Juilliard graduate, but I was finding the path that felt right for me. Of course, I still enjoy my rehearsals and concerts at Carnegie Hall as a member of the New York Pops, a part-time orchestra where I can play with some of the best musicians in New York. However, my passion is sharing how we can use music and vibrations to heal on all levels—body, mind, and spirit—by giving solo concerts and workshops and working privately with individuals.

For many of us, the idea of finding where we fit in seems daunting, if not impossible. Or, we may know where we fit but haven't dared to pursue those goals and dreams. How can we finally take the plunge? These are difficult questions to answer. First, we can start by asking ourselves questions like: where is my growing edge? How can I push myself to expand even further? What will I be talking about next month or in the next year or two? What new goals have I set for myself and what kind of progress will I have made toward achieving those goals?

In other words: What do the lyrics to the soundtrack of your life sound and feel like?

As the themes of your story develop and change, so does the music in its soundtrack. Again, we must ask ourselves the question: what does transformation sound like? For me, I hear music to accompany the most vibrant and gorgeous sunrise. A day opens with every promise that goodness will unfold as new territories are explored. And, when goodness eludes us, the positive changes that we've made allow us to find peace with pain so that we might achieve emotional or spiritual resolution. Transformation is being able to deal with the trials of life in a loving, peaceful, accepting way without fear and pain.

I learned this compelling lesson many years ago from a fortune cookie, of all places, when my most passionate desire was to have a second baby. But, I had an infection that made getting and staying pregnant difficult. I had given birth to a healthy baby girl without too much trouble, but then I had several lost pregnancies. Each month, the wait to find out if I was pregnant felt excruciating.

One night, while eating Chinese food with my husband, I cracked open a fortune cookie which read, "Act as if it has happened until it is proven differently." Because this made sense to me, I decided to prepare for a new baby as if I was already pregnant. My preparation included turning down an opportunity to tour to Japan and Korea with an orchestra because the flying and traveling wouldn't have been good for the early pregnancy. I continued acting "as if" until I finally learned that I was pregnant with our son. I was so elated and thankful, and I learned to "act as if," which sure beats spending that time worrying. As I look back, I see that this was part of the beginnings of this book!

But, sometimes, without knowing how to harness this power, it can also work against you because it involves so much more than willpower.

Years later, during an even more difficult challenge, I realized I was acting "as if" again, but not in a positive way. I was worried about the unthinkable, imagining how I would deal with a terrible situation in the future. My vibration was low, and I definitely didn't have the right tone, imagining every possible negative outcome all on my own. I then realized that I had to be strict with what I allowed my mind to ruminate on during the crisis. I forced myself to see everything resolved and good, to find the high vibration that fits me best and know that the circumstances of my life could be raised to fit that high bar as well. And, everything worked out well!

Our minds are powerful gatekeepers for our lives, and we need to find ways to access the power of the consciousness beneath our thinking minds. I've found visualization to be an incredibly powerful tool. When I look back at some of my biggest miracles, each time I visualized, everything working out. I saw and experienced it "as if" it was already real. I found the right tone, a high vibration which enabled me to feel my desired outcome as already done.

Finding the right tone, the place where we fit into this world, brings connection and joy to our relationships. It provides comfort in times of distress. It gives hope and builds steadfast faith regardless of circumstances. For me, music is that place of connection; the healing power that it brings to so many other people has also healed me as well. Music can also show me my fears, my blocks, and my struggles. I've learned so many lessons in my life through this unending journey with music.

What accompanies you on your journey? Do you have any unrealized passions or goals? For each of us, the resonating pitch, the vibrational level that binds us to our purpose and to those who love us, will be different. Meditate. Ask God to guide you to help you find your passion and purpose. Where do you fit? For many people, this might be a process of seeing signs and answers over time. Once you connect with your passion, share that gift with others in every way possible and by the grace of God. Find the ways to resonate this vibrational pitch and best express your message of love.

EIGHT

THE VIBRATIONAL LEVELS OF HEALING

Miracles can come in all sizes, shapes, and forms. The more we let go and trust in a Higher power, the more miracles will show up in our lives, proving that powerful instant healings are possible in the natural world, like the stories of wondrous healings written about in the Bible. We use the term "miracle" to account for inexplicable occurrences that happen in ways beyond our efforts and abilities. Miracles remind us that a power greater than ourselves exists and can intervene on our behalf, especially when we ask for assistance.

The key is to start looking for and expecting miracles small and large and be grateful for each one. It may be as seemingly insignificant as noticing a favorite bird or the first flower sprouting up through the snow. Or, it can be as big as having cancer go into remission even when the doctors have given up hope. The more you look for and expect divine assistance, the more you'll see it show up in your everyday life. There's nothing to lose by giving it a try. Refunds are allowed if you want your problems back. It's your choice each day, in each moment.

We must remember that, when it comes to divine healing, time doesn't matter; the past, present, and future, are one. So, don't give up if it doesn't happen exactly when and how you feel it necessary. Miracles don't have an expiration date. Clutching onto that kind of score-keeping mentality will just delay your good. Instead of allowing impatience or fear to get the better of you, make the conscious choice to keep living passionately and wholeheartedly. Notice other areas of beauty in your life and appreciate the joy and perfection of the moment. Then, when you least expect it, or perhaps while you are praying fervently, you'll be surprised by how your perfectly orchestrated miracle arrives.

The changes you seek may arrive all of a sudden, or, in parts over time. Sometimes, the miracle may simply be the complete peace and acceptance that one feels, even if the situation itself is unable to completely resolve. The scope of the big picture is beyond our ability to grasp with our limited human perception. Meanwhile, we trust and believe that everything that's needed will be provided for us in divine timing.

Most people have a hard time believing in miracles. Perhaps it's part of a belief system accepted by our collective conscious-ness—the conviction that life must be difficult and that we must earn what we receive through painful experience and sweat equity. We think we need to understand and control our circumstances at all times. More to the point, we've probably been taught that it's irresponsible to not put our efforts into making something happen in a practical, sensible way.

Allowing our needs and desires to be filled in miraculous ways goes against our nature. This is particularly true in the success-driven culture we live in. And, yet, in all our creation sto-ries and religious belief systems, miraculous happenings abound. There's a story in the scripture about Martha and Mary that illustrates this dichotomy. In the Gospel of Luke (10:38-42), Jesus visits the home of Lazarus, Martha, and Mary of Bethany.

The gospel reads: "As Jesus and his disciples were on their way, he came to a village where a woman named Martha opened her home to him. She had a sister called Mary, who sat at the Lord's feet listening to what he said. But, Martha was distracted by all the preparations that had to be made. She came to him and asked, "Lord, don't you care that my sister has left me to do the work by myself? Tell her to help me!" "Martha, Martha," the Lord answered, "you are worried and upset about many things, but only one thing is needed. Mary has chosen what is better, and it will not be taken away from her."

You see, Martha worked very hard while Mary relied on her faith, the thing that could not be taken away. It's hard to see the intrinsic value of relying on faith when we've been taught that we must struggle for everything we get, a belief that might have been passed on through many generations. And, it's true that hard work is indispensable when we want to live a great life. But, if we leave out the spiritual aspect of the equation, I daresay that we've missed the most important part.

The belief in the miraculous is demonstrated throughout the Bible and virtually all other religious texts around the world. But, many of us, whether we consider ourselves believers or not, were taught that it would be arrogant, unrealistic, or even "cultish", if we thought we could expect miracles to show up regularly in our lives. But, what is a miracle except for a spontaneous demonstration of God's love and grace?

The instantaneous healing that occurs when we surrender ourselves to the perfect manifestation of God's wisdom can happen in different ways. But, what's common with any healing is a moment similar to what we call an "ah-ha" moment. "Ah-ha" moments happen when an idea clicks and makes sense; it's a flash of enlightenment that changes everything. Significant, transformational events in our lives often happen in a moment of revelatory awareness. We've all had those once-in-a-lifetime experiences that we can call to mind that gives the proper context to the magnitude of these moments. Our experience with super-learning.

For example, think back on the feeling of opening up the acceptance, or rejection, letter from your dream college. Remember that magical night when you gave or received a marriage proposal from your beloved? Think of the shock of finding out about the illness or passing of a loved one. Or, feel the jolt of understanding from figuring out an answer to a problem that you'd been struggling with for a long time. Whether joyful or traumatic, most life-changing events occur within an instant, usually within ninety seconds or less.

This is how it is with a miracle. It just happens in a moment of revelation: the problem is solved, the prayer is answered, the crooked path is made straight. And, it happens in a way that's beyond the scope of our human limitations. If we worry or try to control and anticipate the exact way a situation should unfold, we don't leave any room for the miracle to occur. But, when we surrender the exact outcome and ask our Higher Power for help, Divine intervention can line up the perfect details for exactly what we desire, at the perfect time. We can anticipate with excitement, believing that we'll receive just what we need when we need it. It's like opening an incredible and priceless gift that's been created especially for you.

Raising your vibrational frequency is an important part of preparing for and receiving a miraculous gift. Just imagine the purity in the sound of a beautiful brass bell. But, if you put a finger on the bell and then try to ring it, you stop the vibrations. This is how the low vibrations of fear, anxiety, control, etc., stop the higher vibrations from ringing and resonating within you. Conversely, each of us is capable of creating miracles in our lives by matching the "right" vibrational frequencies.

When you have a clear and strong image of what you're seeking to experience, it's important to feel as if you've already received it. We create the environment for a miracle to occur by anticipating its arrival with gratitude, excitement, and confidence. Sometimes, a miracle may take a long time to manifest, but the key is to never lose faith. There's more than enough time to experience a miraculous demonstration, as long as we continue to see what we need as already done.

Sometimes, maintaining this level of certainty means we have to increase our vibrational frequency. Dr. David R. Hawkins developed a scale of the frequency levels of what he calls, "consciousness." Dr. Hawkins believed that a vibrational level of 200 is the point at which negative emotions shift to positive ones and force changes to power. His chart, which may be found in his book *Power vs. Force*, is a powerful visual tool for assessing our individual and collective awareness. It is important to notice that even though anger, for instance, is a lower vibrational frequency, don't see it with judgment as being good or bad. The point is that you need to acknowledge, feel, and release it so that you don't stay stuck in a negative cycle. By processing and moving through it and moving on, your vibrational level rises and then you can experience higher levels of peace, joy, and positive manifestations. Remember that unprocessed anger and anxiety affects your health.

However, when a person gets sucked into a negative cycle, it's easy to become trapped there, almost without being aware that it's happened. In fact, one of the reasons it's difficult to shift out of the lower frequencies is because denial and other negative feelings create a vortex of low vibrational frequencies that aim to keep us stuck. But, the choice to become attuned to different vibrational frequencies is ours to make at any time.

As we've discussed previously, everything in the natural world is attuned to a specific frequency, down to the smallest elements of matter. Lung cells have a different vibration than heart cells, which respond to a different vibration than unhealthy cancer cells somewhere else in the body. Likewise, the various organs have different resonant pitches. To envision what this means, imagine yourself in a beautiful cave or a cathedral with a domed ceiling. Shout "hello" and then wait to hear if an echo comes back. As you move around the room and produce different pitches, you'll find that striking the right pitch causes a huge echo to return to you. This would mean that you'd found the most resonant pitch and spot in the space.

When vibrations match the right frequency—be it of a negative core belief or a kidney stone—they can shatter the blockage and cause it to disappear. This is a good visualization to use when you want to release a negative thought pattern or core belief. And, it's one of the most important elements in bringing the body back into a natural state of harmony, calm, and balance. If the human body is in balance, diseased cells can be made "uncomfortable" because the chaotic pattern is now revealed, and the misplaced cells are invited to shift into alignment. Now they can vibrate at a higher resonant pitch that fits into the resounding and resonating chord.

Perhaps you have heard about the thematic energy centers in the body, which are called chakras, in the Ayurvedic system of Indian medicine. Our seven chakras are energy centers, each with a theme and messages for us. It's important that the energy can flow freely within each chakra, as well as throughout the interconnectedness of the seven chakras. Free-flowing energy encourages health and wellbeing, raises our vibrational frequency, and aligns us with the universal energy that births miracles.

Chakras can be referred to as a "place" in our physical body. But, more accurately, they represent the union of our physical body and our soul self. Chakras organize spiritual/soul themes that intersect within the physical body. We connect with the Divine in the core of each of our chakras. But, we also have corresponding organs and bodily systems that emulate the physical manifestation of the soul level. Human beings are a complex system of energy transmitted through our unconscious beliefs, which call forth our conceived options, life choices, and life path. The chakras are pivotal points in this energetic process that move us toward or away from our karmic lessons.

There have been many studies that have sought to quantify these energetic fields. A software company called BioWell Software conducted a successful study to measure them. The study was led in 2013 by Dr. Pradeep B. Deshpande, a professor emeritus at the Department of Chemical Engineering at the University of Louisville. According to Dr. Deshpande, it's possible to quantitatively estimate the energy of the chakras.

Dr. Deshpande compared the chakras of two participants in his case studies and demonstrated the contrast in a chart. The first participant was asked to engage in meditation and breathing practices and to focus their thoughts on love and kindness, which produced perfectly aligned chakras corresponding to their calm, relaxed, and healthy energy field. It was full, complete, and vibrant, with the balanced and aligned chakras resonating at high frequency. The second participant was unhealthy and emotionally unbalanced, whose corresponding chart showed the chakras completely misaligned with most of them outside of the body, and the surrounding energy field was filled with gaps.

Each chakra has a different resonant pitch, which the vibrations can find. The fourth chakra is located near the heart. It is known to have the largest electromagnetic field, which processes energetically communicated emotional information. Much of this energetic communication is based on our subconscious beliefs and patterns. People respond one way when they feel and communicate love, compassion, or gratitude. By comparison, when our vibrations communicate negative messages such as hatred and fear, we have a different reaction. As we use the exercises we're learning, to tune-up, align, and balance each chakra, we'll resonate from a place of love and wholeness.

Spontaneous changes and healing can happen by using vibrations to find the resonant pitch within each chakra. The right vibrations shift the dissonance into harmony. But, I believe that the resonant pitch of a chakra, organ, or even a thought, isn't a generalized note for all people in all conditions. Resonant pitch changes with each individual, even from moment to moment. We can use exercises, however, to help us find the most effective pitch for our individual bodies and circumstances.

The Toning Release Exercise helps to clear, balance, and align the chakras. Begin by sitting comfortably, closing your eyes with your feet connected to the ground. Take a deep breath in through the nose, pause, and then breathe out through the mouth while releasing a vowel sound with a long slow exhale. Feel the vibrations connect and tune into the chakra that you're focused on. It's most helpful if you experiment with different vowel sounds. These vowel sounds are suggestions that work well. This exercise is listed with a set of variables that can be added, one at a time. Begin with the lowest chakra and the lowest sound that you can release; it can be raspy and rough. Each time you do this chakra alignment, choose a chakra and what aspect you feel inspired to focus on, for instance, the mantra, color, and movement for the first three chakras. Or, let each moment invite you to the next.

For the exhale, tone using a different vowel for each chakra. As you are toning, listen and connect to the resonant pitch, this is when the sound feels the fullest, perhaps the loudest. You aren't preparing to sing an opera in front of an audience, so do your best not to feel self-conscious about how these noises sound. This is a personal, intimate, sacred experience as the vibrations you emit help clear and tune to your soul's sounds.

After you've completed the toning for a chakra, say an affirmation, a mantra, while holding an image of the chakra spinning freely with the color associated with that chakra. Remember that color is also a form of energy.

The following mantras are specifically geared to activating the highest vibratory frequency within each specific energy field. These meditations are a perfect way to tune-up and maintain your resonance and alignment.

First: root chakra, use "UH;" start with the lowest guttural sound that you can produce. See RED. MANTRA: I am worthy to exist. Element: Earth. Theme: Ancestral, letting go, basic trust. Rocks, clay, and bells.

Second: sacral chakra, use "OOH;" (for each chakra, let the pitch become higher). See ORANGE. I am worthy to feel and create. Element: Water; Theme: Creation, acceptance. Rose flower essence.

Third: solar plexus chakra, use "OH;" remember, the pitch rises as you move higher in the body. See YELLOW. I am worthy to be who I am meant to be. Element: Fire. Theme: Self-esteem, wisdom, and power. Breath work.

Fourth: heart chakra, use "AH;" See GREEN. I am worthy to give and receive love. Element: Air; Theme: Love and healing. Rose Quartz.

Fifth: throat chakra, use "I;" See BLUE (sapphire or indigo). I am worthy to speak, express myself, and be heard. Element: Ether. Theme: Communication, truth. Chanting.

Sixth: 3rd eye chakra, use "A;" See DEEP PURPLE. I am worthy to see the truth. Element: Thought. Theme: awareness, intuition, and insight. Visualization.

Seventh: sacral crown chakra, use "EE." See WHITE. I am worthy of Divine knowing (universal truth and connection). Element: Light. Theme: Spirituality, knowing, and Oneness. Meditation.

Another option is to add visualization. As you vocalize and focus on balancing each chakra, in your mind's eye, see and hear a differently sized brass bell ringing. The bell needs to be free of any debris, dust, or interference in your mind to ring freely—do this in your imagination. A difference can be heard, seen, and felt, when the bell is no longer muffled by interference. The larger the bell, the lower the sound. For instance, the first chakra has the largest bell, and each bell gets progressively smaller, and higher, in your mind as you move up the chakras.

The purpose of the toning exercise is to clear, clean, and tune each chakra. Then, see the image of bells ringing as you do the toning release on the vowels, which activate and attune the balancing vibrations. In the end, in your mind and body, imagine the sound of all the tones freely ringing out together. Hear and feel all of the bells ringing in harmony. Keep in mind that the chakras are all intertwined, and one affects the others. Clearing and balancing the chakras is important to be in alignment and in tune.

The different aspects of this exercise speak to the levels of healing that can be attained through the tuning process. Just as healing happens in layers, life happens as a series of events. Though the most transformational, foundational events happen in a moment, many other occurrences are based on that initial event. Whether thematically positive or negative, each event forms another layer confirming the dominant belief. In other words, if your dominant belief is that "the universe is for me and miracles abound in my life," then that's what you're most likely to experience.

Our lives and relationships are based on these beliefs, and our reaction to circumstances either confirm or deny them. Over time, as we're willing to maintain our healing journey, it can become a pleasant process to watch positive changes occur progressively. It starts to feel natural to have the energy centers in our bodies aligned and vibrating at high levels. Being "in tune" becomes our normal state, creating the space for miracles to manifest with ease and grace.

We've already discussed some of the techniques that change or raise the vibration to facilitate healing and miracles at the deepest levels. Once again, those include:

> *Breathwork*: Feel the divine energy that surrounds you as you inhale. Feel the vibrations travel through your nose, down to your chest and then back again as you exhale. Feel the cleansing vibrations release the mental and emotional blockages you don't need. While seated, close your eyes, lightly place your thumb on your fingers and imagine receiving all the gifts that God has to offer on the in-breath. Then, release all of your blocks on the out-breath, leaving you in a state of forgiveness and gratitude.

> *Tapping*: Tapping, is also known as EFT or Emotional Freedom Techniques. This is another tool that can help you subtly activate vibrations and changes. There are many wonderful books and information online about EFT that go into depth on the use of the technique as well as the science and psychology behind the practice. But, for now, as a quick introduction, just know that EFT is a form of psychological acupressure, based on the same energy meridians used in traditional acupuncture to treat physical and emotional ailments. It draws on various theories of alternative medicine including acupuncture, neuro-linguistic programming, energy medicine, and Thought Field Therapy. EFT, or tapping, is designed to quickly and easily release negative emotions and core beliefs. To use EFT, start by thinking of what you're releasing. Then, say affirmations claiming your new, replacement beliefs as you tap on different energy meridian points. Tap on the top of your head, between your eyebrows, the side of your eyes, under your eyes, under your nose, on your chin, the collarbone, under the arm and do a karate chop as you tap the side of both hands together.

> *Drumming*: Collect whatever drums and percussion instruments you can find. If you feel like you need some help for rhythmic guidance, listen to a soundtrack that speaks to you while you drum on your favorite instrument. You can drum using only your instrument, or add some bells, a rattle, or a gong. The percussive energy will help you express what you want to release,j and change and then find a way to bring in and reinforce the circumstances that you want to experience instead. This is an incredibly fun exercise that you can build on in many ways. Create your theme song, add your voice or use some "body percussion" remebering that you are an instrument. Above all, have fun!

> *Intention setting*: Now that you realize that you're the master of your fate, the hero of your story, continue to take time

to create the detailed, sensory experiences that will move you forward. Envision how you want things to be in your life and set the clear intention to make it to your goals. Invite God to help you on your quest, to guide you into right action. Know that you are worthy of everything good!

> *Tune in and tune up*: As often as you can, pause, tune in, and use your breath to shift yourself into a high-frequency state of harmony and balance. Use the exercises that work best for you to help you do this. In a balanced state, we are calm, our body knows how to be healed and whole, and we can express true happiness!

> *Use movement*: Dancing or moving your body to certain rhythms is a spiritual practice that helps you focus on "being" in your body. It allows creativity to direct the expression and flow of the body as it finds connection and moves within a community of dancers. This is a simple process that invites deep, on-going explorations while routing out self-conscious limitations and isolation. Unhindered movement allows people to tap into new depths of connection with themselves and others. Each rhythm is expressed and experienced in a uniquely personal way. This opens a new sense of freedom and possibility, invites healing and inspiration while also being deeply restorative.

I once saw a video clip of a deer just after he barely escaped an attack by a wolf. Before running away, he shook himself off to release the tension and fear. Human beings tend to hold onto our pain and fear for far too long. Our bodies remember the events of our lives, especially the painful ones. When we move, it helps to unthaw and release this tension. Instead of holding on, allow the rhythm of your life to dance through your cells, your bones, and your being. Let your elbow, foot, head, or knee be the leader.

Put on different kinds of music. Feel the flow of life energy move through every part of you. Let energy be "emotion," or energy in motion. Start by expressing jagged, staccato, defined movements, like an angry and free march with stomping and release anger as a child does; feel your beautiful body flow through space, let the emotions come up and through you as you gradually begin to flow through space.

Feel yourself move higher and then lower, fast and very slowly. Be still and wait until you make your next decided move. Feel your arms dance gracefully through space creating a melody within the body. Move in an unorganized, jagged, messy way. Feel yourself be like a wave blown about by the wind, floating. Have fun! When you are ready, rest in stillness and gratitude for all the ways your body serves you.

There are so many fun, easy, and practical ways to tie all this information together so that it can be used in your daily life. Pay attention to the music of your heart. The real power is in the spaces between the notes, the breaths, the words, the thoughts; that miraculous space of divine possibility is what matters the most. The silence that lives there is like a painter's blank canvas before the painting has begun—it can become anything.

Without silence, there could be no music, no miracles. Silence is being at peace, allowing yourself to be divinely guided rather than frantically pursuing whatever comes your way, good or bad. Stop and listen to the sounds you hear. What is the difference between sound and silence? Could we hear a sound without the silence between? Is there silence between your questions and answers?

Sound is born from silence. You must embrace the silence from within yourself to hear the messages. We're all united by a vibrating string of Universal energy that connects us to All That Is. This connection gives us the ability to hear more than the sound. We can hear the beauty and complexity that is the masterpiece—the soundtrack—to our soul's work and journey. And, that is the greatest miracle of all.

NINE
RESONANT PITCH

Human beings are the physical manifestation of God's love. This intrinsic connection to our Creator is the reason we can be both the instrument and the musician in God's orchestra; the music we make becomes the soaring notes of the symphony and the silence between phrases. To listen to this music from a place of meditative emptiness is to feel your soul's center as it exists beyond personality and the ego's needs. It is to call forth the beauty, peace, and love, as we move toward the spiritual wisdom that surpasses our human understanding.

Though our music lives deep within us, and though its expression is very personal, its manifestation is not about us. If we personalize the experience, we limit it. If we seek to process this demonstration on a human plane, it becomes two dimensional and circular. But, if we embrace the universal, the process becomes three dimensional; it starts within ourselves and then it goes out in every direction, connecting us all at the most fundamental level.

I believe this concept of Oneness is explained most beautifully by string theory—the idea that we're connected to each other by similar vibrating strings. The strings of the viola illustrate what happens when we align ourselves in harmonic resonance. When one note is played, the sympathetic tones and overtones are also activated, and they vibrate along with the initial tone, supporting it. Similarly, when we pause, listen, and adjust, we can feel the sympathetic resonance and support of the universe as it magnifies and vibrates with us in harmony.

The SoundPath principles we've learned suggest new ways of thinking and living that allow us to readily tune in to the higher vibrations. It's a new lifestyle based on faith instead of fear, and harmony instead of discord. Tuning up the mind and body creates balance and a renewed sense of clarity. If you've gone through life feeling like you're not enough, or striving to earn the approval of others, the SoundPath tools will raise your confidence and increase your peace of mind.

Using sound and vibration therapy, coupled with the additional techniques like meditation, can bring healing and fulfillment to any person who's willing to harness the power of this method. Everyone knows that music can change their mood and most people have songs or different playlists to do just that. Even our colloquialisms reflect the recognition that music plays a fundamental part in our relationships. I'm sure you've heard people say they were able to "strike a chord" with someone. Or, they'll say they've "played someone's heartstrings." There's no coincidence in the use of words like this.

String theory, or the "Theory of Everything," explains the interconnectedness of our natural world in ways that other scientific theories cannot. Since all matter is made up of tiny vibrating strands of energy, the particular pattern of the string's vibration makes one particle of matter or an object different than another. It's within this framework of energy and vibration that we can communicate on every level—not just in the traditional ways we're used to sharing with each other.

The scientific basis of string theory is obviously complex, but I try to summarize it for myself by visualizing the image of a vibrating string, connecting me to the Creator of All that Is. The connection goes through my heart, tuning and aligning all my chakras, and then grounding me to the center of the earth. I call this visualization process *SoulString Alignment.* In workshop settings, I use specific sounds to reinforce the images of connecting to the vibrating string. I visualize the vibrating string connected to the core of the earth, which then passes through all of my chakras. Then, the top of the string is connected to heaven.

The bottom of the string centered in the earth is connected to a very low frequency which is called the Schumann resonance. It is believed to be fundamental to the nature of this planet, our "bass note", which everything is based on. You can think of it as the heartbeat of the earth. Called a tuning fork for life, it influences the biological circuitry of the mammalian brain—our nervous system. The ancient Indian, Rishis, referred to this as OHM, the incarnation of pure sound. This pitch is much lower than the range of the human ear.

The hot molten iron in the center of the Earth shoots strong electromagnetic pulses into outer space from the South Pole. Those pulses then curl around the Earth due to the attraction of the Earth's North Pole, where they re-enter the Earth. The pulses thereby form a cacoon around the Earth that protects us from radiation from the Sun. "Schumann resonance" measures the electromagnetic pulses in the Earth's ionosphere, inside this cacoon. The main frequency has usually been found at 7.83 Hz, also associated with low levels of the alpha brain wave state and the upper range of the theta brain wave state. Although that requency is inaudible to the human ear, in 2017 the Schumann main resonance frequency sometimes reached as high as 36+ Hz, thus at times it can correspond to a musicial note, between an "A" and a "D".

Some people believe that connecting with this frequency helps to align your energy with the earth's energy. It takes the premise behind string theory and makes it emotionally accessible to the average person in ways that make sense in their lives.

My application of the string theory, which I call *SoulString Alignment,* focuses on expanding the concept that all matter, including ourselves, is comprised of vibrating strings at a core level. We want to consciously connect to those vibrating strings, which emanate what we've come to believe about who we are and how loveable, capable, and worthwhile we are. We want to communicate using vibrations—the language of energy that our subconscious mind speaks. We also want to invite our Higher Power to be the "conductor" of these symphonic dialogues.

There are seven spiritual principles behind *SoulString Alignment*; they can be remembered by the acronym, S.T.R.I.N.G.S. These seven letters summarize the steps to take to find your SoundPath to freedom. My CD, *SongPath*, was created to accompany these steps.

S.T.R.I.N.G.S. can give us a road map to follow on our journey to freedom. It can keep us on course, so we don't take detours or get lost along the way. The first step is to:

Surrender your struggles. When we've been carrying heavy burdens throughout our lives, we might not even be aware that things could change and be easier. We don't have to do it alone, relying on our efforts. Surrendering our struggles doesn't mean that we're giving up and we have to admit failure and defeat. It's the opposite. Instead, we're realizing that what we're dealing with is too much for anyone, and we agree to accept an easier way.

Trust in a power greater than yourself. Many people feel that they need to control the circumstances of their lives, especially when things are going bad. Maybe thinking about a power greater than yourself even brings up negative experiences or thoughts. But, it's virtually impossible to move forward without acknowledging that we all need help from time to time and being willing to receive it. You can keep it very simple. Start by admitting that you'd like things to be easier and have better results. Then, acknowledge that what you've been doing is exhausting and not always effective, especially when it involves other people.

Review, realize and release. First, stop and take an inventory of what feels right and what doesn't in your life. Then, once you realize what you want to release, apply the SoundPath practices and exercises to help you let go of those life-long negative habits and core beliefs. Ask your Higher Power for help and use the Serenity Prayer whenever you need to: *God grant me the SERENITY to accept the things I cannot change, the COURAGE to change the things I can, and the WISDOM to know the difference.* This process of release also includes asking your Higher Power to help you forgive and release any grudges, resentments, or regrets you may hold from experiences where you felt you'd been wronged.

Insights, Inspiration and Intuition. Being in tune offers great rewards as you move through your days. Some call this place of inspiration "being in the zone." It's where we feel ease and flow as life unfolds. Clarity of mind enables us to hear the voice of God speaking. Webster's Dictionary defines intuition as "the ability to understand something without the need for conscious reasoning." This aligns with one of the main goals of SoundPath—connecting to the subconscious mind. Intuition clears the space for insights we might have missed if we were stuck in a dissonant, chaotic state of mind, struggling to fight our battles on our own. Inspiration provides the means for acting on those insights and revelations.

New Pathways allow you to negate the negative. Build new habits and neural pathways. Neural pathways are a preferred course for sending energy symbols connecting one part of the brain to another. Because neurons are dynamic and can change, the brain can adapt to changing circumstances. This is called neuroplasticity, and it explains how we develop new pathways in the brain, which can happen after a stroke or brain injury. Imagine it as reprogramming a computer's hard drive or bypassing software that's filled with bugs and downloading a new, updated version. Perhaps this may require that you create a system to check on your progress. You may want to "red flag" particular thoughts or habits. You may decide to make a habit of checking at certain times of the day and remembering to tune-in, breathe, and listen to the sounds around you to clear your mind. Negate the negative by replacing it with the positive options that lead to new choices and opportunities.

Gratitude leads to more of God's Grace. Give thanks to God for our gifts including the gift of grace. This is one of the best habits we can practice. It's so important to acknowledge and appreciate all you have. Being grateful also positions us to receive more of what we're grateful for. Have you ever been excited to send someone a gift, but instead of returning the excitement with a heartfelt thank you, the person never even acknowledged having received it? Would this inspire you to repeat this generosity the next time you have the opportunity? I believe if we're not grateful for the gifts we've already been given, we interrupt the flow of receiving more good into our lives. Being in a state of appreciation feels good and opens the door to experiencing more of the same. When we're given miracles, we haven't earned them and don't necessarily deserve them. They truly are gifts given to us by grace. But, being greedy and always expecting another "favor" stems from a much lower vibrational state. Make sure that even when you go about a busy day, take time to be grateful for all beauty and magic that has brightened your path along the way. If possible, make a practice of stopping throughout the day to thank God for something wonderful in your world. Getting into a practice of giving gratitude allows us to be in a state of receiving grace.

Serenity, silence and sharing. Being in a state of serenity and stillness offers so many rewards. Letting go of the incessant daily struggle opens up an oasis of peace. Silence and meditation give the mind space to rest, which allows for greater clarity and insights. When we have the grace to know this state of surrender, we come full circle as the questions become answers. The real key to profound serenity is to share what we've learned and what we have with others who are in need. It's said that we can only keep what we give away. However, there's a catch to this philosophy. There's an art to giving that involves finding a way to give from your overflow rather than from a deficit.

The two ways of giving may look similar, yet they're very different, and the difference isn't detectable with the human eye. It lies on the subconscious level, within one's intention and the reason for giving. Giving from the overflow means sharing with others from the bounty of your blessings because you are a kind, compassionate, generous, empathic person. It does not mean giving to the point where you or your family members have to go without. And, it also does not mean giving with the expectation of getting a specific return on your investment. These habits don't create win-win situations. But, sharing from the overflow is the surest way to keep you in-tune and resonating your truth.

If you're helping someone because you feel obligated, or it would be too uncomfortable to say no, or because it makes you feel needed, the help may not be well-received. In these cases, the intention to give comes more from the head and the ego than from the heart. This also applies to close family members who may appear to be struggling. If we give out of desperation with the hope that things will turn out the way we want it to, we're giving with an intention to control and manipulate. This is why some of our best intentions can be taken as interfering and have the opposite effect than we'd hoped. But, when God is part of the equation, our service is magnified to create the best possible outcome for all concerned.

Using the S.T.R.I.N.G.S. tools to tune up your life generates more possibilities than you could ever imagine. You are a beautiful instrument. Negative experiences don't define who you are; they provide platforms for you to leap from as you move higher. Hopefully, by now it's clear that music and vibrations provide an important key for tapping into those magical and miraculous paths to spiritual and emotional liberation.

SoundPath assists with healing on the deepest levels—even in hidden places in the psyche. At our core, we're all energetic beings, and we come from the same universal energy as everything else in creation. When we're able to use sound vibrations to engage this energy, we can finally dislodge our most profound pains and disappointments, shifting discord into resolution.

The key to the kingdom lies within yourself. You are singing the notes; the tones that reverberate through your life arise from within, connecting and expressing the truth of who you are when you sing. No one else can sing your song with your signature qualities. You may look to others for advice and help, but no one can accept or experience healing for you.

Your healing is connected to your relationship with a Higher Power; be willing to go to God and ask for help. This is quite a different approach than living in a state of panic, feeling like everything is a matter of life and death. No one would knowingly choose to live in this state. However, many people do because they don't know a better way. But, the truth is that you have all of the necessary tools to live in a place of positivity and joy where miracles happen regularly.

So, which way will you choose to go? Are you choosing life or are you choosing a slow death? Why not choose each day to accept the vibrant and amazing life you were born to lead? Experience true health in your mind, body and spirit as you resonate in harmony and happiness.

Years ago, I endured a pretty nasty health scare. I'd been given a cancer diagnosis, and in the months that followed, I spent a fair share of time thinking about when I would die. I had many conversations with God about my time here, my goals, and the work that I am dedicated to accomplishing. I believe that whenever the time comes, I will see God and be surrounded by unexplainable beauty. But, in the intervening years, I want to give a hundred and ten percent of myself, so that when I enter heaven, I'll know that I did everything possible to develop my gifts and ability to serve others. My ability to focus on being in alignment allows my body to heal and function in the miraculous ways that it knows how to do. Today, I celebrate my good health.

However, during my time of healing from cancer, I chose to take an inventory of my life and ask some difficult questions: had I chosen, with humility and guidance, to help those in need? Had I learned and grown when faced with the difficult challenges, or did I choose to stay the same? Have I left a positive impact on those coming behind me? How much love was I able to give? How much love was I able to receive? Did I love myself at least as much as I have loved others, as it says in the Bible?

When I asked these questions, the insights I received told me exactly what areas of my life I needed to focus on. If you ask yourself the same questions, the answers will take you to a deeper state of awareness where you can connect to the highest source of all—God.

The message of this book is about taking control of your life and your destiny, being your own hero. We're all capable of using music and vibrations, a language communicated through energy, to fill any gaps and clear up any confusion in our lives. When we raise our vibration by using sound therapy combined with the S.T.R.I.N.G.S. principles, pain and disappointment can be replaced with a sense of wholeness, unconditional love, calm, courage, clarity, and purpose.

But, to arrive at this place of harmony, you must let go of control. It's up to you to request the help and guidance from a power greater than yourself. Tune-in, tune-up, and listen to your intuition, which will lead you to receive gifts from above that are far greater than any you could have dreamed. This undertaking isn't easy, but miracles abound on this path.

Sound opens consciousness. So, think in sound. Let rhythm be your inner pulse, connecting you to universal life. Let music lead you to your inner story. See past the memories of pain you re-lived because of negative programming. Only then can you heal and move on to create joyful, new memories, allowing your vibrational energy to carry you to higher places.

Please visit www.karenolson.com to learn about available SoundPath Method programs and to sign up for free enewsletters.